SCHOLASTIC

25 Complex Text Passages to Meet the Common Core

Literature and Informational Texts

Grade 4

by Martin Lee and Marcia Miller

NEW YORK ● TORONTO ● LONDON ● AUCKLAND ● SYDNEY
MEXICO CITY ● NEW DELHI ● HONG KONG ● BUENOS AIRES

Teaching *Resources*

Cover design: Scott Davis
Interior design: Kathy Massaro

Interior illustrations: Teresa Anderko, Delana Bettoli, and Mike Moran © 2014 by Scholastic Inc.

Image credits: page 30 © Tsurukame Design/Shutterstock, Inc.; page 46 (top) © Aksenova Natalya/Shutterstock, Inc.; page 46 (bottom) © prapass/Shutterstock, Inc.; page 54 © Scott Cornell/Shutterstock, Inc.; page 56 © plamen petrov/Big Stock Photo; page 58 © DLILLC/Media Bakery; page 60 © AP Images; page 64 (top) © SlipFloat/Shutterstock, Inc.; page 66 (top) © sahua d/Shutterstock, Inc.; page 66 (bottom) © Julio Aldana/Shutterstock, Inc.; page 72 © Carlos S. Pereyra/Media Bakery; page 74 © Saagar Patel/Hacker Scouts.

ISBN: 978-0-545-57710-6
Copyright © 2014 by Scholastic Inc.
All rights reserved.
Printed in the U.S.A.
Published by Scholastic Inc.

8   9   10   40   21   20   19   18

Contents

"To build a foundation for college and career readiness, students must read widely and deeply from among a broad range of high-quality, increasingly challenging literary and informational texts. Through extensive reading of stories, dramas, poems, and myths from diverse cultures and different time periods, students gain literary and cultural knowledge as well as familiarity with various text structures and elements. By reading texts in history/social studies, science, and other disciplines, students build a foundation of knowledge in these fields that will also give them the background to be better readers in all content areas. Students can only gain this foundation when the curriculum is intentionally and coherently structured to develop rich content knowledge within and across grades. Students also acquire the habits of reading independently and closely, which are essential to their future success."

—COMMON CORE STATE
STANDARDS FOR ENGLISH
LANGUAGE ARTS, JUNE 2010

25 Complex Text Passages to Meet the Common Core: Literature and Informational Texts—Grade 4 includes complex reading passages with companion comprehension question pages for teaching the two types of texts—Literature and Informational—covered in the Common Core State Standards (CCSS) for English Language Arts. The passages and lessons in this book address the rigorous expectations put forth by the CCSS "that students read increasingly complex texts through the grades." This book embraces nine of the ten CCSS College and Career Readiness Anchor Standards for Reading that inform solid instruction for literary and informational texts.

Anchor Standards for Reading

Key Ideas and Details

1. Read closely to determine what the text says explicitly and make logical inferences from it; cite specific textual evidence when writing or speaking to support conclusions drawn from the text.

2. Determine central ideas or themes of a text; summarize key supporting details and ideas.

3. Analyze how and why individuals, events, and ideas develop and interact throughout a text.

Craft and Structure

4. Interpret words and phrases as they are used in a text, including determining technical, connotative, and figurative meanings, and analyze how specific word choices shape meaning or tone.

5. Analyze the structure of texts, including how specific sentences, paragraphs, and larger portions of text relate to each other and the whole.

6. Assess how point of view or purpose shapes the content and style of a text.

Integration of Knowledge and Ideas

7. Integrate and evaluate content presented in diverse media and formats, including visually and quantitatively, as well as in words.

8. Delineate and evaluate the argument and specific claims in a text, including the validity of the reasoning as well as the relevance and sufficiency of the evidence.

Range of Reading and Level of Text Complexity

10. Read and comprehend complex literary and informational texts independently and proficiently.

The materials in this book also address the Foundational Standards for Reading, including skills in phonics, word recognition, and fluency as well as Language Standards, such as the conventions of standard English, knowledge of language, and vocabulary acquisition and use. In addition, students meet Writing Standards as they answer questions about the passages, demonstrating their ability to convey ideas coherently, clearly, and with support from the text. On page 12, you'll find a correlation chart that details how the 25 passages meet specific standards. This information can also be found with the teaching notes for each passage on pages 13–25.

About Text Complexity

The CCSS recommend that students tackle increasingly complex texts to develop and hone their skills and knowledge. Many factors contribute to the complexity of any text.

Text complexity is more intricate than a readability score alone reveals. Most formulas examine sentence length and structure and the number of difficult words. Each formula gives different weight to different factors. Other aspects of text complexity include coherence, organization, motivation, and any prior knowledge readers may bring.

A complex text can be relatively easy to decode, but if it examines complex issues or uses figurative language, the overall text complexity rises. By contrast, a text that uses unfamiliar words may be less daunting if readers can apply word-study skills and context clues effectively to determine meaning.

This triangular model used by the CCSS shows three distinct yet interrelated factors that contribute to text complexity.

CCSS Model of Text Complexity

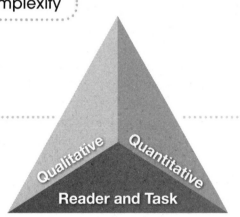

Qualitative measures consider the complexity of meaning or purpose, structure, language conventionality, and overall clarity.

Quantitative measures complexity in terms of word length and frequency, sentence length, and text cohesion. Lexile® algorithms rank this type of complexity on a numerical scale.

Reader and Task considerations refer to such variables as a student's motivation, knowledge, and experience brought to the text, and the purpose, complexity, and types of questions posed.

About the Passages

The 25 reproducible, one-page passages included in this book are divided into two categories. The first 9 passages represent literature (fiction) and are followed by 16 informational texts (nonfiction). Each grouping presents a variety of genres and forms, organizational structures, purposes, tones, and tasks. Consult the table of contents (page 3) to see the scope of genres, forms, and types of content-area texts. The passages within each category are arranged in order of Lexile score (the quantitative measure), from lowest to highest, and fall within the Lexile score ranges recommended for fourth graders. The Lexile scores for grade 4, revised to reflect the more rigorous demands of the CCSS, range from 740 to 940. For more about complexity level determinations, see page 5 and pages 8–9.

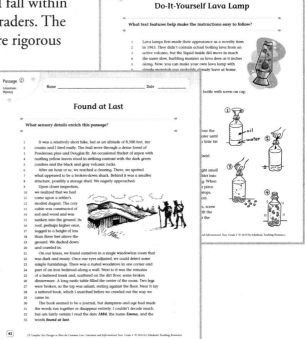

Each passage appears on its own page beginning with the title, the genre or form of the passage, and an opening question to give students a focus to keep in mind as they read. Some passages also include visual elements, such as photographs, drawings, illustrations, or tables, as well as typical text elements, such as italics, boldface type, bulleted or numbered lists, subheadings, or sidebars.

The line numbers that appear to the left of each passage will help you and your students readily locate a specific line of text. For example, students might say, "I'm not sure how to pronounce the name here in line 5." They might also include line numbers to identify text evidence when they answer questions about the piece. For example: "The author says in lines 11–13 that…"

The passages are stand-alone texts and can be used in any order you choose. Feel free to assign passages to individuals, small groups, or the entire class, as best suits your teaching style. However, it's a good idea to preview each passage before you assign it, to ensure that your students have the skills needed to complete it successfully. (See page 10 for a close-reading routine to model for students.)

About the After-Reading Question Pages

The Common Core standards suggest that assessment should involve "text-dependent questions." Questions constructed to meet this demand guide students to cite evidence from the text. They fall into three broad categories: 1) Key Ideas and Details, 2) Craft and Structure, and 3) Integration of Knowledge and Ideas. According to the standards, responses should include claims supported by the text, connections to informational or literary elements found within the text explicitly or by logical implication, and age-appropriate analyses of themes or topics.

Following each passage is a reproducible page with five text-dependent comprehension questions for students to answer after reading. Two are multiple-choice questions that call for a single response and a brief text-based explanation to justify that choice. The other questions are open response items. These address a range of comprehension strategies and skills. Students can revisit the passage to find the evidence they need to answer each question. All questions share the goal of ensuring that students engage in close reading of the text, grasp its key ideas, and provide text-based evidence in their answers. In addition, the questions are formatted to reflect the types of questions that will be asked on standardized tests. The questions generally proceed from easier to more complex:

✳ The **least challenging** questions call for basic understanding and recall of details. They involve referencing the text verbatim or paraphrasing it. This kind of question might also ask students to identify a supporting detail an author did or did not include when making a persuasive argument.

✳ The **mid-level** questions call upon students to use mental processes beyond basic recall. To answer these questions, students may need to use context clues to unlock the meaning of unfamiliar words and phrases (including figurative language), classify or compare information, make inferences, distinguish facts from opinions, or make predictions. Such a question might also ask students to summarize the main idea(s) of a passage.

✳ The **deeper** questions focus on understanding that goes beyond the text. Students may need to recognize the author's tone and purpose, make inferences about the entire passage, or use logic to make predictions. This kind of question might even call upon students to determine why an author began or ended the passage as he or she did.

You may find it useful to have students reference line numbers from the passage for efficiency and clarity when they formulate answers. They can also refer to the line numbers during class discussions. Provide additional paper so students have ample space to write complete and thorough answers.

An answer key (pages 76–80) includes sample answers based on textual evidence and specific line numbers from the passage that support the answers. You might want to review answers with the whole class. This approach provides opportunities for discussion, comparison, extension, reinforcement, and correlation to other skills and lessons in your current plans. Your observations can direct the kinds of review and reinforcement you may want to add to subsequent lessons.

About the Teaching Notes

Each passage in this book is supported by a set of teaching notes found on pages 13–25.

In the left column, you will see the following features for each set of teaching notes.

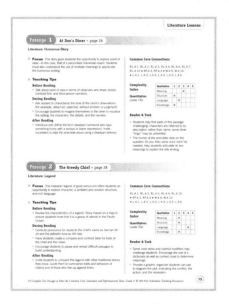

* Grouping (**Literature** or **Informational Text**) and the genre or form of the piece.

* **Focus** statement describing the essential purpose of the passage, its main features, areas of emphasis, and what students will gain by reading it.

* **Teaching Tips** to help you motivate, support, and guide students before, during, and after reading. These easy-to-use suggestions are by no means exhaustive, and you may choose to add or substitute your own ideas or strategies.

- **Before Reading** tips include ways to introduce a passage, explain a genre, present a topic, discuss a format, introduce key vocabulary, or put a theme in context. A tip may suggest how to engage prior knowledge, connect with similar materials in other curriculum areas, or build motivation.

- **During Reading** tips offer possible procedures to help students work through the text, ideas for highlighting key words or concepts, suggestions for graphic organizers, and so on.

- **After Reading** tips provide follow-up questions, discussion topics, extension activities, further readings, or writing assignments linked to the text.

In the right column, are the essential CCSS connections for the passage sorted according to the specific sections of the document: **RL** (Reading Standards for Literature) or **RI** (Reading Standards for Informational Text), **RF** (Reading Standards: Foundational Skills), **W** (Writing Standards), and **L** (Language Standards). The CCSS chart on page 12 provides the correlations for the entire book at a glance and a URL for the CCSS website where you can find the specific wording of each skill.

Under the essential CCSS connections, you will find a **Complexity Index**, which offers analytical information about the passage based on the three aspects of text complexity, briefly summarized on the next page.

* **Quantitative** value, represented by a Lexile score.
* **Qualitative** rating, which appears in a matrix that presents four aspects of this measure:

  * **Meaning** for literary texts (single level of meaning ↔ multiple levels of meaning) or **Purpose** for informational texts (explicitly stated purpose ↔ implicit purpose)
  * **Structure** (simple ↔ complex organization; simple ↔ complex graphics)
  * **Language** (literal ↔ figurative; clear ↔ ambiguous; familiar ↔ unusual; conversational ↔ formal)
  * **Knowledge** (life experience; content expectations; cultural or literary background needed)

Each of the above aspects are ranked from 1 to 5, briefly summarized, as follows:

1	2	3	4	5
Simple, clear text; accessible language, ideas, and/or structure	Mostly linear with explicit meaning/purpose; clear structure; moderate vocabulary; assumes some knowledge	May have more than one meaning/purpose; some figurative language; more demanding structure, syntax, language, and/or vocabulary; assumes some knowledge	Multiple meanings/purposes possible; more sophisticated syntax, structure, language, and/or vocabulary; assumes much knowledge	May require inference and/or synthesis; complex structure, syntax, language, and/or vocabulary; assumes extensive knowledge

* **Reader and Task** considerations comprise two or more bulleted points. Ideas relating to the reader appear first, followed by specific suggestions for a text-based task. Reader and Task considerations also appear embedded within the teaching notes as well as in the guiding question that opens each passage and in the comprehension questions. Keep in mind that Reader and Task considerations are the most variable of the three measures of text complexity. Reader issues relate to such broad concerns as prior knowledge and experience, cognitive abilities, reading skills, motivation by and engagement with the text, and content and/or theme concerns. Tasks are typically questions to answer, ideas to discuss, or activities to help students navigate and analyze the text, understand key ideas, and deepen comprehension. The same task may be stimulating for some students but daunting to others. Because you know your students best, use your judgment to adjust and revise tasks as appropriate.

Teaching Routine to Support Close Reading

Complex texts become more accessible to readers who are able to use various strategies during the reading process. One of the best ways to scaffold students through this process is to model a close-reading routine.

✳ **Preview the text.** Help students learn to identify clues about the meaning, purpose, or goal of the text. They can first read the title and the guiding question that precedes the passage. In literary texts, students can scan for characters' names and clues about setting and time frame. In informational texts, students can use features such as paragraph subheadings and supporting photos, illustrations, or other graphics to get a sense of the organization and purpose.

✳ **Quick-read to get the gist.** Have students do a "run-through" individual reading of the passage to get a sense of it. The quick-read technique can also help students identify areas of confusion or problem vocabulary. You can liken this step to scanning a new store to get a sense of how it is set up, what products it sells, and how you can find what you need.

✳ **Read closely.** Next, have students read the same piece again, this time with an eye to unlocking its deeper meaning or purpose. For most students, this is the time to use sticky notes, highlighter pens, margin notes, or graphic organizers to help them work their way through the important parts of the text. You might provide text-related graphic organizers, such as T-charts, compare/contrast and Venn diagrams, character and concept maps, cause-and-effect charts, or evidence/conclusion tables.

✳ **Respond to the text.** Now it's time for students to pull their ideas together and for you to assess their understanding. This may involve summarizing, reading aloud, holding group discussions, debates, or answering written questions. When you assign the after-reading question pages, suggest that students reread questions as needed before they attempt an answer. Encourage them to return to the text as well. Remind students to provide text-based evidence as part of every answer. Finally, consider with students the big ideas of a piece, its message, lesson, or purpose, and think about how to extend learning.

Above all, use the passages and teaching materials in this book to inspire students to become mindful readers—readers who delve deeply into a text to get the most out of it. Help your students recognize that reading is much more than just decoding all the words. Guide them to dig in, think about ideas, determine meaning, and grasp messages.

The following page presents three copies of a reproducible, six-step guide to mindful reading. It is intended as a reusable prompt. Students can keep it at hand to help them recall, apply, and internalize close-reading strategies whenever they read.

25 Complex Text Passages to Meet the Common Core: Literature and Informational Texts, Grade 4 © 2014 by Scholastic Teaching Resources

How to Be
A Mindful Reader

Preview the text.
- Set a purpose for reading.

Read carefully.
- Slow down and stay focused.
- Monitor your understanding.

Read again.
- You might notice new information.

Take notes.
- Mark difficult words or phrases.
- Write questions in the margin.
- Make connections between ideas.

Summarize.
- Add headings.
- Jot down the main ideas.
- List the events in sequence.

Think about it.
- Read between the lines. What's the message?
- Do you agree or disagree?
- Has anything been left out?

How to Be
A Mindful Reader

Preview the text.
- Set a purpose for reading.

Read carefully.
- Slow down and stay focused.
- Monitor your understanding.

Read again.
- You might notice new information.

Take notes.
- Mark difficult words or phrases.
- Write questions in the margin.
- Make connections between ideas.

Summarize.
- Add headings.
- Jot down the main ideas.
- List the events in sequence.

Think about it.
- Read between the lines. What's the message?
- Do you agree or disagree?
- Has anything been left out?

How to Be
A Mindful Reader

Preview the text.
- Set a purpose for reading.

Read carefully.
- Slow down and stay focused.
- Monitor your understanding.

Read again.
- You might notice new information.

Take notes.
- Mark difficult words or phrases.
- Write questions in the margin.
- Make connections between ideas.

Summarize.
- Add headings.
- Jot down the main ideas.
- List the events in sequence.

Think about it.
- Read between the lines. What's the message?
- Do you agree or disagree?
- Has anything been left out?

Connections to the Common Core State Standards

As shown in the chart below, the teaching resources in this book will help you meet many of the reading, writing, and language standards for grade 4 outlined in the CCSS. For details on these standards, visit the CCSS website: www.corestandards.org/the-standards/.

Passage	Reading: Literature							Reading: Informational Text								Reading: Foundational Skills		Writing		Language					
	RL.4.1	RL.4.2	RL.4.3	RL.4.4	RL.4.6	RL.4.7	RL.4.10	RI.4.1	RI.4.2	RI.4.3	RI.4.4	RI.4.5	RI.4.7	RI.4.8	RI.4.10	RF.4.3	RF.4.4	W.4.9	W.4.10	L.4.1	L.4.2	L.4.3	L.4.4	L.4.5	L.4.6
1	●	●	●	●	●	●	●									●	●	●	●	●	●	●	●	●	●
2	●	●	●	●			●									●	●	●	●	●	●	●	●	●	●
3	●	●	●	●		●	●									●	●	●	●	●	●	●	●	●	●
4	●	●	●	●		●	●									●	●	●	●	●	●	●	●	●	●
5	●	●	●	●			●									●	●	●	●	●	●	●	●	●	●
6	●	●	●	●		●	●									●	●	●	●	●	●	●	●	●	●
7	●	●	●	●		●	●									●	●	●	●	●	●	●	●	●	●
8	●	●	●	●	●	●	●									●	●	●	●	●	●	●	●	●	●
9	●	●	●	●		●	●									●	●	●	●	●	●	●	●	●	●
10								●	●	●	●	●	●		●	●	●	●	●	●	●	●	●	●	●
11								●	●	●	●	●		●	●	●	●	●	●	●	●	●	●	●	●
12								●	●		●	●		●	●	●	●	●	●	●	●	●	●	●	●
13								●	●		●	●		●	●	●	●	●	●	●	●	●	●	●	●
14								●	●		●	●		●		●	●	●	●	●	●	●	●	●	●
15								●	●	●	●	●	●	●	●	●	●	●	●	●	●	●	●	●	●
16								●	●	●	●	●	●	●	●	●	●	●	●	●	●	●	●	●	●
17								●	●		●	●		●	●	●	●	●	●	●	●	●	●	●	●
18								●	●	●	●	●	●	●	●	●	●	●	●	●	●	●	●	●	●
19								●	●	●	●	●	●	●	●	●	●	●	●	●	●	●	●	●	●
20								●	●	●	●	●	●		●	●	●	●	●	●	●	●	●	●	●
21								●	●	●	●	●	●	●		●	●	●	●	●	●	●	●	●	●
22								●	●		●	●	●	●	●	●	●	●	●	●	●	●	●	●	●
23								●	●	●	●		●	●	●	●	●	●	●	●	●	●	●	●	●
24								●	●		●			●	●	●	●	●	●	●	●	●	●	●	●
25								●	●		●	●	●		●	●	●	●	●	●	●	●	●	●	●

At Don's Diner • page 26

Literature: Humorous Story

▶ **Focus** This story gives students the opportunity to explore point of view—in this case, that of a personified inanimate object. Students must also understand the use of multiple meanings to appreciate the humorous ending.

▶ **Teaching Tips**

Before Reading
• Talk about point of view in terms of observers who share details. Contrast first- and third-person narrators.

During Reading
• Ask readers to characterize the tone of the clock's observations (for example, *detached, objective, without emotion or judgment*).
• Encourage students to imagine themselves in the diner to visualize the setting, the characters, the details, and the narrator.

After Reading
• Introduce and define the term *deadpan* (someone who says something funny with a serious or blank expression). Invite volunteers to read the anecdote aloud using a deadpan delivery.

Common Core Connections

RL.4.1, RL.4.2, RL.4.3, RL.4.4, RL.4.6, RL.4.7, RL.4.10 • RF.4.3, RF.4.4 • W.4.9, W.4.10
• L.4.1, L.4.2, L.4.3, L.4.4, L.4.5, L.4.6

Complexity Index

Quantitative: Lexile 740

Qualitative	1	2	3	4	5
Meaning			✳		
Structure	✳				
Language		✳			
Knowledge	✳				

Reader & Task

• Students may find parts of this passage challenging: characters are referred to by description rather than name; some diner "lingo" may be unfamiliar.
• The humor of the anecdote rests on the question *Do you folks serve duck here?* As needed, help students articulate its two meanings to explain the silly ending.

Passage 2   **The Greedy Chief** • page 28

Literature: Legend

▶ **Focus** This Hawaiian legend of good versus evil offers students an opportunity to explore character, a problem-and-solution structure, and rich language.

▶ **Teaching Tips**

Before Reading
• Review the characteristics of a legend. Show Hawaii on a map to ensure students know that it is a group of islands in the Pacific Ocean.

During Reading
• Correctly pronounce for students the chief's name as *hah-lah-AY-ah* and the yellowfin tuna as *AH-hee*.
• Have students create a compare-and-contrast table for traits of the chief and the crews.
• Encourage students to pause and reread difficult passages to build understanding.

After Reading
• Invite students to compare this legend with other traditional stories they know. Guide them to summarize traits and behaviors of villains and of those who rise up against them.

Common Core Connections

RL.4.1, RL.4.2, RL.4.3, RL.4.4, RL.4.10
• RF.4.3, RF.4.4 • W.4.9, W.4.10
• L.4.1, L.4.2, L.4.3, L.4.4, L.4.5, L.4.6

Complexity Index

Quantitative: Lexile 760

Qualitative	1	2	3	4	5
Meaning		✳			
Structure		✳			
Language				✳	
Knowledge		✳			

Reader & Task

• Some vivid verbs and colorful modifiers may challenge students. Encourage the use of a dictionary as well as context clues to determine meanings.
• Provide a graphic organizer students can use to diagram the plot, indicating the conflict, the action, and the resolution.

Literature: Realistic Fiction

▶ **Focus** This piece asks students to analyze the traits of the main character and her teacher, and follow the changes the main character undergoes as she faces a challenging task.

▶ **Teaching Tips**

Before Reading
- Review key narrative elements: plot, setting, character, conflict, and resolution.
- Preview some of the physical education terms (for example, *gymnastics*, *vault*, *Swedish box*, and *spotter*).

During Reading
- Suggest that students pause at the end of each paragraph to summarize or sketch Greta's attitude at that point in the story.
- Have students study the photo and caption to help visualize the gymnastics apparatus described in the story.

After Reading
- Invite students to respond to the story by relating it to other texts they know in which a character overcomes a daunting challenge.

Common Core Connections

RL.4.1, RL.4.2, RL.4.3, RL.4.4, RL.4.7, RL.4.10
- RF.4.3, RF.4.4 • W.4.9, W.4.10
- L.4.1, L.4.2, L.4.3, L4.4, L.4.5, L4.6

Complexity Index

Quantitative: Lexile 780

Qualitative	1	2	3	4	5
Meaning		❊			
Structure		❊			
Language			❊		
Knowledge		❊			

Reader & Task

- Most students will respond and relate to a situation in which a student fears a worrisome task.
- Encourage students to picture themselves as Greta and as Mr. Lin as they read about the conflict and resolution. Have them predict what will happen at different junctures.

Literature: Tall Tale

▶ **Focus** This tall tale from Colorado lets students identify the features typical of tall tales: exaggeration, absurdity, humor, and folksy wit.

▶ **Teaching Tips**

Before Reading
- If possible, show pictures of trout, 19th century mining camps, itinerant peddlers, and so-called "snake-oil" salesmen.
- Review the typical elements of tall tales (exaggeration, humor, absurdity).

During Reading
- Have students circle words or expressions that may be new or unclear.
- To help build oral fluency, invite volunteers to read this tall tale aloud as if they were an old timer entertaining friends around a campfire.

After Reading
- Encourage students to compare this tale to other tall tales they may know.
- Invite students to write their own tall tales using humor, exaggeration, and colorful language.

Common Core Connections

RL.4.1, RL.4.2, RL.4.3, RL.4.4, RL.4.7, RL.4.10
- RF.4.3, RF.4.4 • W.4.9, W.4.10
- L.4.1, L.4.2, L.4.3, L.4.4, L.4.5, L.4.6

Complexity Index

Quantitative: Lexile 790

Qualitative	1	2	3	4	5
Meaning		❊			
Structure		❊			
Language			❊		
Knowledge			❊		

Reader & Task

- Students who are unfamiliar with pioneer life and itinerant peddlers may have difficulty envisioning the setting.
- The absurdities inherent in the tale may be a challenge for some students. Have them use text markings to indicate which aspects are realistic, exaggerated, or absurd.

Literature: Folktale

▶ **Focus** In this folktale from Nigeria, enriched by the use of figurative language and vivid verbs, students identify the style and elements of a "pourquoi" tale.

▶ **Teaching Tips**

Before Reading

• Review other examples of folktales, myths, or legends that attempt to explain why the world is as it is.

During Reading

• Have students characterize Chief Eyo based on his actions.

• Encourage students to highlight descriptive words and phrases used to illustrate the movements of the ants and the worms.

After Reading

• To help students distinguish between the factual and fictional characteristics of the ants in the story, help them research the unique skills of driver, guard, and scout ants. They might also investigate the scientific reason for why worms live underground.

Common Core Connections

RL.4.1, RL.4.2, RL.4.3, RL.4.4, RL.4.10
• RF.4.3, RF.4.4 • W.4.9, W.4.10
• L.4.1, L.4.2, L.4.3, L.4.4, L.4.5, L.4.6

Complexity Index

Quantitative: Lexile 820

Qualitative	1	2	3	4	5
Meaning		✲			
Structure		✲			
Language				✲	
Knowledge		✲			

Reader & Task

• Students may or may not be familiar with pourquoi tales. Explain that *pourquoi* is a French word meaning *why*. Pourquoi tales are fictional stories that explain why or how a fact of nature came to be.

• Tell students to summarize the folktale, and then suggest possible answers to the question that precedes the passage.

Literature: Fable

▶ **Focus** This fable from Aesop challenges students to understand its moral and navigate both literal and figurative language.

▶ **Teaching Tips**

Before Reading

• Review the characteristics of a fable and its summarizing lesson, or moral.

During Reading

• Encourage students to mark unfamiliar words, phrases, or ideas to research or discuss later. Have them also highlight examples of descriptive language and alliteration.

After Reading

• Challenge students to develop modern retellings of the fable with a different main character that faces another frustrating experience and departs with bitterness.

Common Core Connections

RL.4.1, RL.4.2, RL.4.3, RL.4.4, RL.4.7, RL.4.10
• RF.4.3, RF.4.4 • W.4.9, W.4.10
• L.4.1, L.4.2, L.4.3, L.4.4, L.4.5, L.4.6

Complexity Index

Quantitative: Lexile 830

Qualitative	1	2	3	4	5
Meaning			✲		
Structure		✲			
Language				✲	
Knowledge			✲		

Reader & Task

• Engage prior knowledge of fables from Aesop and other cultural traditions.

• Encourage students to think about the events of this fable with an eye to understanding the meaning of its moral.

Literature: Fantasy

▶ **Focus** Students explore the features of a fantasy in this account of a boy's dream about special agents from the future that possess super powers.

▶ **Teaching Tips**

Before Reading
- Review the meaning of fantasy, and invite students to give examples of works of fantasy that they have read or seen.

During Reading
- Encourage students to reread sentences or paragraphs as necessary to clarify their understanding of challenging vocabulary and concepts.
- Tell students to highlight words and phrases that signal the passage is written in the first person.

After Reading
- Challenge students to explain how they inferred that the events in the passage were part of the boy's dream.
- Facilitate an online visit to the real International Spy Museum in Washington, D.C., to help students get a better sense of what visitors can experience there.
- Have students write a paragraph in which they create their own fantasy special agent and describe his or her challenges (problems) and abilities (solutions).

Common Core Connections

RL.4.1, RL.4.2, RL.4.3, RL.4.4, RL.4.7, RL.4.10
• RF.4.3, RF.4.4 • W.4.9, W.4.10
• L.4.1, L.4.2, L.4.3, L.4.4, L.4.5, L.4.6

Complexity Index

Quantitative:
Lexile 840

Qualitative	1	2	3	4	5
Meaning			✷		
Structure			✷		
Language			✷		
Knowledge				✷	

Reader & Task

- The futuristic special agents and their abilities will engage most students though some may be unfamiliar with the topic of special agents and spies.
- Encourage students to describe the fantastical elements in this passage and explain how each special agent's abilities helped him or her prevent danger.

Literature: Historical Fiction

▶ **Focus** This story, told through the recollections of a fictional child, offers students a glimpse into an actual historical event of great significance.

▶ **Teaching Tips**

Before Reading
- Provide background information about the history of women's rights in America, as needed.
- Compare and contrast a nonfiction historical text and historical fiction.

During Reading
- Encourage students to use context clues to figure out the meaning of unfamiliar words, such as *chuffed*, *tyranny*, and *noggin*.

After Reading
- Have students compare and contrast this piece with other examples of historical fiction they have read.

Common Core Connections

RL.4.1, RL.4.2, RL.4.3, RL.4.4, RL.4.6, RL.4.7, RL.4.10 • RF.4.3, RF.4.4 • W.4.9, W.4.10
• L.4.1, L.4.2, L.4.3, L.4.4, L.4.5, L.4.6

Complexity Index

Quantitative:
Lexile 890

Qualitative	1	2	3	4	5
Meaning				✷	
Structure			✷		
Language				✷	
Knowledge				✷	

Reader & Task

- Some historical persons and events, vocabulary, and sentence structures may challenge students.
- Understanding the distinction between a fictional and nonfictional historical account may be a challenge for some students.
- Instruct students to highlight details in the passage that could be factual and then confirm by research.

Literature: Mystery

▶ **Focus** This brief mystery, rich with sensory details, focuses on descriptive vocabulary, setting, and the puzzle of a surprising discovery.

▶ **Teaching Tips**

Before Reading

- Preview the piece by reading its opening paragraph aloud to students. Ask them to explain what they visualize about the setting.

During Reading

- Encourage students to highlight sensory details that bring the setting to life.

After Reading

- Invite students to generate possible explanations about who built the cabin, why it was located there, why it was abandoned, and who Emma may have been.

Common Core Connections

RL.4.1, RL.4.2, RL.4.3, RL.4.4, RL.4.7, RL.4.10 • RF.4.3, RF.4.4 • W.4.9, W.4.10 • L.4.1, L.4.2, L.4.3, L.4.4, L.4.5, L.4.6

Complexity Index

Quantitative:
Lexile 930

Qualitative	1	2	3	4	5
Meaning			✳		
Structure			✳		
Language				✳	
Knowledge					✳

Reader & Task

- Urban students may have little familiarity with mountain hiking. Others may be able to link details in this story with prior knowledge of pioneer life.
- Have students jot down questions as they read about the setting, the cabin, the objects in it, who may have lived there, and what may have happened to them.

Passage 10 — Frogs on Logs • page 44

Informational Text: Procedural/Recipe

▶ **Focus** This simple recipe uses text elements (bulleted lists, numbered list, subheadings, illustrations) to enable readers to follow a sequence of steps successfully.

▶ **Teaching Tips**

Before Reading
- Tell students that they will read a procedural piece of writing called Frogs on Logs. Have them study the two illustrations, and then predict what the piece may be about.
- Invite students to share what they know about recipes: what they are, why people use them, and how they convey information.

During Reading
- Guide students to identify the distinctions among sections in the recipe.
- Have students connect the illustration near the bottom of the page with the written information in the text.

After Reading
- To help students better appreciate why a recipe is broken down into parts and sequential steps, guide small groups to make Frogs on Logs to share. (Check for food allergies ahead of time.) Ask: *How would the outcome change if the steps were not in order?*
- Challenge students to come up with a no-cook snack recipe and write an informational text that explains how to make it using the Frogs on Logs recipe as a model.

Common Core Connections

RI.4.1, RI.4.2, RI.4.3, RI.4.4, RI.4.5, RI.4.7, RI.4.10 • RF.4.3, RF.4.4 • W.4.9, W.4.10
• L.4.1, L.4.2, L.4.3, L.4.4, L.4.5, L.4.6

Complexity Index

Quantitative: Lexile 740

Qualitative	1	2	3	4	5
Purpose	✳				
Structure		✳			
Language	✳				
Knowledge		✳			

Reader & Task

- Students who have never helped prepare food may be unfamiliar with the conventions of following a recipe.
- Relate following a recipe to similar experiences students may have had, such as following the directions for playing a game or conducting a science experiment.

Passage 11 — "Citizen" of the World • page 46

Informational Text: Magazine Article

▶ **Focus** In this passage, written in the style of a magazine article, students encounter social studies terms and concepts, and navigate subheadings—nonfiction text features that help organize the text.

▶ **Teaching Tips**

Before Reading
- Talk with students about how the structure and tone of a magazine article differ from those of other kinds of informational writing.
- Provide a world map students can use to locate the places mentioned.

During Reading
- The opening paragraph is written as a riddle to entice readers. Encourage students to circle text evidence that helps answer it.
- Have students explain how the boldfaced subheadings can guide their reading.
- This passage contains words with suffixes (for example, *originally*, *flightless*, *broilers*). Suggest that students highlight them for analysis after reading.

After Reading
- Invite students to research the significance of other animals in cultures throughout history (for example, cats, cows, horses), and choose one to write an informational article about.

Common Core Connections

RI.4.1, RI.4.2, RI.4.3, RI.4.4, RI.4.5, RI.4.8, RI.4.10 • RF.4.3, RF.4.4 • W.4.9, W.4.10
• L.4.1, L.4.2, L.4.3, L.4.4, L.4.5, L.4.6

Complexity Index

Quantitative: Lexile 750

Qualitative	1	2	3	4	5
Purpose			✳		
Structure			✳		
Language			✳		
Knowledge			✳		

Reader & Task

- Some social studies concepts and vocabulary may challenge students.
- Encourage students to summarize the main points of the piece using the subheadings as a guide.

Informational Text: e-mail Letter

▶ **Focus** In this letter, written as a friendly e-mail, students identify aspects of the writer's character, including his attitudes and interests. They also identify elements of a sincere and useful apology.

▶ **Teaching Tips**

Before Reading
- Clarify that an e-mail is a letter written, sent, and received in electronic form. Display an e-mail to model its standard format.
- Check that students know the meaning of *apology*. Brainstorm circumstances that might require an apology, and the appropriate tone and language to use.

During Reading
- This passage contains words with prefixes (for example, *reschedule*, *unexpected*) and suffixes (*eventually*, *sincerest*). Suggest that students highlight them for analysis during reading.

After Reading
- Invite students to draft a letter that Ms. Lopez might write in response to the apology.

Common Core Connections

RI.4.1, RI.4.2, RI.4.4, RI.4.5, RI.4.8, RI.4.10 • W.4.9, W.4.10 • L.4.1, L.4.2, L.4.3, L.4.4, L.4.5, L.4.6

Complexity Index

Quantitative: Lexile 760

Qualitative	1	2	3	4	5
Purpose	✻				
Structure	✻				
Language	✻				
Knowledge	✻				

Reader & Task

- The casual tone of this e-mail will help make it accessible to many students.
- Have students make a character map of Marcus that identifies his qualities and interests that can be inferred from his e-mail.

Informational Text: Persuasive Speech

▶ **Focus** Students analyze the components of a persuasive speech in which the speaker offers a proposal and supports it with evidence and explanation aimed specifically at his audience.

▶ **Teaching Tips**

Before Reading
- Brainstorm with students features that make a good speech or oral presentation.

During Reading
- Ask a volunteer to read the speech aloud with expression as Devin might, with classmates as the school board audience.
- Instruct students to note main ideas by paragraph.

After Reading
- Encourage students to return to the text to highlight details that identify how Devin grabs his audience, addresses listeners' interests, represents students, and ends with impact.

Common Core Connections

RI.4.1, RI.4.2, RI.4.4, RI.4.5, RI.4.8, RI.4.10 • RF.4.3, RF.4.4 • W.4.9, W.4.10 • L.4.1, L.4.2, L.4.3, L.4.4, L.4.5, L.4.6

Complexity Index

Quantitative: Lexile 770

Qualitative	1	2	3	4	5
Purpose	✻				
Structure		✻			
Language		✻			
Knowledge	✻				

Reader & Task

- Most students will respond to the idea of a student suggesting a school improvement.
- Help students analyze the speech, paragraph by paragraph, to evaluate its success as a persuasive tool.

Informational Text: Brochure

▶ **Focus** This example of technical writing presents information with various text and graphical features in the form and style of a brochure.

▶ **Teaching Tips**

Before Reading

- Introduce the term *brochure* and, if possible, display sample brochures from local businesses, schools, activity centers, and so on. Identify common features.
- Clarify that a brochure is a kind of advertisement that gives key details likely customers need in order to make choices.

During Reading

- As necessary, guide students to read every section, including the opening, to determine the kind of information each provides.

After Reading

- Have student groups critique the brochure for clarity, completeness of information, and style. Encourage them to offer suggestions for improvement.
- Invite students to use this passage as a model to create their own activity brochure on a real or imaginary topic.

Common Core Connections

RI.4.1, RI.4.2, RI.4.4, RI.4.5, RI.4.7, RI.4.10 •
RF.4.3, RF.4.4 • W.4.9, W.4.10
• L.4.1, L.4.2, L.4.3, L.4.4, L.4.5, L.4.6

Complexity Index

Quantitative:
Lexile 780

Qualitative	1	2	3	4	5
Purpose		✳			
Structure				✳	.
Language		✳			
Knowledge		✳			

Reader & Task

- Students may not have had experience finding information in a brochure or pamphlet.
- Guide students to identify the brochure's key details they need to know to participate in one or more activity groups: day, subject, time, number of meetings, group size.

Informational Text: Interview

▶ **Focus** Students read an interview, written in a question-and-answer format, in which a child poses a variety of questions to an adult who has an unusual job.

▶ **Teaching Tips**

Before Reading

- Discuss what an interview is and how the person asking the questions might prepare in advance to get the best information.
- Read the title together. Then have students predict what they think this interview will be about.

During Reading

- Guide students to notice how the structure of this passage differs from other types of writing. (For example: *It is an interview organized in a Q & A format, boldface letters distinguish the interviewer and the person being interviewed; and the questions are in italics to set them off*).
- Refer students to the photo for a better sense of a flight team at work.

After Reading

- Invite students to formulate additional questions they wish they could ask Carlos to learn more about balloon wrangling. Extend by having students research answers to their questions using online resources.

Common Core Connections

RI.4.1, RI.4.2, RI.4.4, RI.4.5, RI.4.7, RI.4.8,
RI.4.10 • RF.4.3, RF.4.4 • W.4.9, W.4.10
• L.4.1, L.4.2, L.4.3, L.4.4, L.4.5, L.4.6

Complexity Index

Quantitative:
Lexile 790

Qualitative	1	2	3	4	5
Purpose		✳			
Structure		✳			
Language			✳		
Knowledge			✳		

Reader & Task

- Many students will be familiar with huge parade balloons, but may never have considered the responsibilities and challenges their handlers face.
- Encourage students to evaluate each interview question for the kind of information it elicits.

Informational Text: Memoir

▶ **Focus** Students will explore cause-and-effect and character in this memoir about an unforgettable childhood event.

▶ **Teaching Tips**

Before Reading

- Explain that a memoir is a kind of autobiography in which the writer explains how an event or person affected his or her life.
- Discuss with students what it means to tune a piano. Tell them to study the photograph to see how a piano looks inside. If possible, show them the intricate interior of an actual piano.

During Reading

- Correctly pronounce the piano tuner's name as *RO-zhak*.
- Invite students to "storyboard" the memoir as a way to visualize and remember it.

After Reading

- Have students describe how the author reacted to Mr. Rožak at work. Also challenge them to pose questions they might ask the tuner, if they could.

Common Core Connections

RI.4.1, RI.4.2, RI.4.3, RI.4.4, RI.4.5, RI.4.7, RI.4.8, RI.4.10 • RF.4.3, RF.4.4 • W.4.9, W.4.10 • L.4.1, L.4.2, L.4.3, L.4.4, L.4.5, L.4.6

Complexity Index

Quantitative:
Lexile 800

Qualitative	1	2	3	4	5
Purpose			✳		
Structure		✳			
Language			✳		
Knowledge			✳		

Reader & Task

- Some students may not understand the concept of tuning a piano, or realize that someone who is visually impaired can develop strong job skills.
- Focus students on understanding the impact this experience had on the writer and how it changed this person's life.

Informational Text: Persuasive Essay

▶ **Focus** Students identify the elements of a logical and well-organized argument in this essay that makes a case for an unlikely proposal.

▶ **Teaching Tips**

Before Reading

- Discuss features of a good persuasive essay, such as a forceful introduction, point-by-point arguments, acknowledgement of opposing views, and a strong closing.

During Reading

- Invite students to offer reasons why the title has a question mark.
- Tell students to highlight details in the passage that demonstrate how the writer uses humor to make his points. Discuss reasons humor can be an effective tool when trying to persuade someone to agree with you.

After Reading

- Have students identify the arguments the writer presents by stating the main idea of each paragraph, and then evaluate the effectiveness of the arguments.
- Challenge students to suggest other positive arguments and problems the writer did not mention.

Common Core Connections

RI.4.1, RI.4.2, RI.4.4, RI.4.5, RI.4.8, RI.4.10 • RF.4.3, RF.4.4 • W.4.9, W.4.10 • L.4.1, L.4.2, L.4.3, L.4.4, L.4.5, L.4.6

Complexity Index

Quantitative:
Lexile 810

Qualitative	1	2	3	4	5
Purpose			✳		
Structure			✳		
Language			✳		
Knowledge		✳			

Reader & Task

- The lighthearted tone of this piece will engage students, and many will be amused and intrigued by the notion of bringing pets to school.
- Have students analyze how the essay is organized by jotting down key words in the margins to track the writer's argument.

Informational Text: Newspaper Article

▶ **Focus** This newspaper article requires students to navigate nonfiction text features and interpret baseball lingo to understand a remarkable and surprising historic event.

▶ **Teaching Tips**

Before Reading

- Tell students that newspaper sports articles are often colorfully written to engage readers and are typically filled with sports-specific slang and idioms.
- Explain that Babe Ruth and Lou Gehrig were two of the most legendary baseball players of all time. Also clarify the meaning of baseball terms, such as *spring training, exhibition game, minor league, sluggers, rookie, mound,* and *commissioner.*

During Reading

- If possible, have students read the passage in small groups that include at least one person with baseball knowledge to help the others with any unfamiliar vocabulary not yet discussed. You might also invite an advanced reader to read it aloud with expression.

After Reading

- Encourage students to describe why the piece may have been challenging to them, for example: Did they have enough knowledge of the topic? Did they have trouble visualizing what was being described? Was the style of the writing interesting and engaging or not? Was the vocabulary, the syntax, and the genre clear?

Common Core Connections

RI.4.1, RI.4.2, RI.4.3, RI.4.4, RI.4.5, RI.4.7, RI.4.8, RI.4.10 • RF.4.3, RF.4.4 • W.4.9, W.4.10 • L.4.1, L.4.2, L.4.3, L.4.4, L.4.5, L.4.6

Complexity Index

Quantitative: Lexile 830

Qualitative	1	2	3	4	5
Purpose				✳	
Structure				✳	
Language					✳
Knowledge				✳	

Reader & Task

- Students who lack knowledge of baseball and its terms and expressions will likely need support.
- To help students synthesize the information in the newspaper article, have them retell the account in their own words or present it as a skit.

Informational Text: Problem-Solution Essay/Table

▶ **Focus** Readers use information presented in the text and on a calendar to solve a realistic scheduling problem.

▶ **Teaching Tips**

Before Reading

- Inform students that they will read information in text form and use a calendar to solve a scheduling problem. Review calendar terminology and organization as needed.

During Reading

- Have students mark up the calendar to indicate dates of conflict for each friend. When finished, they can circle all available dates that remain.

After Reading

- Challenge students to use this passage as a model to write their own text with calendar-based problems for classmates to solve.

Common Core Connections

RI.4.1, RI.4.2, RI.4.4, RI.4.5, RI.4.7, RI.4.8, RI.4.10 • RF.4.3, RF.4.4 • W.4.9, W.4.10 • L.4.1, L.4.2, L.4.3, L.4.4, L.4.5, L.4.6

Complexity Index

Quantitative: Lexile 850

Qualitative	1	2	3	4	5
Purpose				✳	
Structure			✳		
Language			✳		
Knowledge				✳	

Reader & Task

- Some students may have difficulty determining a logical way to solve the problem.
- Encourage students to verbalize how they were able to use the information in the text to figure out possible dates for Juan's party.

Informational Text: Procedural/Science Activity

▶ **Focus** Readers follow sequential directions in text and lists to learn how to do a science activity using common household materials.

▶ **Teaching Tips**

Before Reading
- Have students explain why it's important to read all the information given before undertaking a science project.

During Reading
- Tell students to highlight any unclear terms or steps. Discuss and clarify later.
- Suggest that students link the materials to the steps that use them.

After Reading
- Discuss how the illustrations support each step in the instructions.
- Gather sufficient materials so that groups can follow the directions to make lava lamps.

Common Core Connections

RI.4.1, RI.4.2, RI.4.3, RI.4.4, RI.4.5, RI.4.7, RI.4.10 • RF.4.3, RF.4.4 • W.4.9, W.4.10 • L.4.1, L.4.2, L.4.3, L.4.4, L.4.5, L.4.6

Complexity Index

Quantitative: Lexile 860

Qualitative	1	2	3	4	5
Purpose			✳		
Structure			✳		
Language				✳	
Knowledge			✳		

Reader & Task

- Students who have never done a DIY project from written instructions may need additional support.
- To help students better appreciate why the text is broken down into parts and sequential steps, ask: *How would the outcome change if the steps were not in order?*

Informational Text: Cultural Article

▶ **Focus** Readers compare and contrast two Aztec calendars and relate them to the modern calendar we use today.

▶ **Teaching Tips**

Before Reading
- Inform students that the Aztecs lived in Mexico long ago, but their civilization has largely vanished. If possible, display some images of Aztec art or historic sites. Explain that millions of Mexicans today are descended from the Aztecs.

During Reading
- Encourage students to use the subheadings and graphic elements to aid in comprehension.
- Suggest that students make margin notes with questions to discuss later.

After Reading
- Help students make a concept map for each of the Aztec calendars, and one for our modern calendar. Discuss similarities and differences.

Common Core Connections

RI.4.1, RI.4.2, RI.4.3, RI.4.4, RI.4.5, RI.4.7, RI.4.10 • RF.4.3, RF.4.4 • W.4.9, W.4.10 • L.4.1, L.4.2, L.4.3, L.4.4, L.4.5, L.4.6

Complexity Index

Quantitative: Lexile 880

Qualitative	1	2	3	4	5
Purpose				✳	
Structure		✳			
Language					✳
Knowledge					✳

Reader & Task

- Some historical and cultural concepts and vocabulary may challenge students.
- The structure and organization of this passage will aid students in comparing and contrasting the two Aztec calendars described in the text.

Informational Text: Compare & Contrast Essay/Table

▶ **Focus** Readers gather information from descriptive text and a data comparison table to make a sensible purchasing decision.

▶ **Teaching Tips**

Before Reading

• Provide basic background about the Wright brothers' historic first flight and the tragic sinking of the HMS *Titanic*. Display photos if possible.

During Reading

• Encourage students to highlight text details about Wesley—his interests and abilities—to guide their thinking about which model he should choose.

• Tell students to explain why the table presents descriptive text, numbers, and symbols.

After Reading

• With adult supervision, have students research model kits online to explore the types and formats of the assembly instructions they provide.

Common Core Connections

RI.4.1, RI.4.2, RI.4.4, RI.4.5, RI.4.7, RI.4.8, RI.4.10 • RF.4.3, RF.4.4 • W.4.9, W.4.10 • L.4.1, L.4.2, L.4.3, L.4.4, L.4.5, L.4.6

Complexity Index

Quantitative: Lexile 890

Qualitative	1	2	3	4	5
Purpose				✲	
Structure					✲
Language			✲		
Knowledge				✲	

Reader & Task

• Some students may find the multipart comparison table challenging.

• Help students integrate the information provided and the options to propose a sensible decision for Wesley to make.

Informational Text: Biographical Sketch

▶ **Focus** Students read about the unexpected start, the stellar rise, and the character of a young chess champion through narrative and quotations from the subject himself.

▶ **Teaching Tips**

Before Reading

• Review the features of a biography with students. Discuss the value of including direct quotations to reveal character traits or attitudes.

• Explain that *blitz chess* is a game of chess played with little time to think over one's moves.

During Reading

• Instruct students to scan the piece before close reading and notice how the subheadings help organize the chronological structure.

• Encourage students to reread sentences or paragraphs as needed for full comprehension.

• As they read, students can list questions to ask or comments to discuss later.

After Reading

• Invite students to use evidence from the text to explain why Josh Waitzkin is an interesting subject for such a biographical sketch.

Common Core Connections

RI.4.1, RI.4.2, RI.4.3, RI.4.4, RI.4.5, RI.4.8, RI.4.10 • RF.4.3, RF.4.4 • W.4.9, W.4.10 • L.4.1, L.4.2, L.4.3, L.4.4, L.4.5, L.4.6

Complexity Index

Quantitative: Lexile 900

Qualitative	1	2	3	4	5
Purpose			✲		
Structure			✲		
Language					✲
Knowledge					✲

Reader & Task

• Students unfamiliar with the world of chess may find this passage challenging.

• Have students use the subheadings as a guide in summarizing the unusual circumstances of Josh Waitzkin's entry into the chess world.

Informational Text: Letter to the Editor

▶ **Focus** Readers examine a letter to the editor, a type of persuasive writing that uses a problem-solution format to respond to another point of view.

▶ **Teaching Tips**

Before Reading
- Show students examples of letters to the editor from a local newspaper and discuss their purpose and common features.
- To address challenging vocabulary, review useful word-analysis techniques.

During Reading
- Encourage students to look for context clues to determine word meanings.
- Tell students to highlight the details and reasons put forth by the writer to persuade readers to adopt his point of view.

After Reading
- Have students explain how well the writer made a case for preserving the theater.
- Invite students to debate the pros and cons of restoring an old structure or tearing it down to build something new. If possible, link the situation in the letter to a similar one in your area.

Common Core Connections

RI.4.1, RI.4.2, RI.4.3, RI.4.4, RI.4.5, RI.4.8, RI.4.10 • RF.4.3, RF.4.4 • W.4.9, W.4.10 • L.4.1, L.4.2, L.4.3, L.4.4, L.4.5, L.4.6

Complexity Index

Quantitative: Lexile 910

Qualitative	1	2	3	4	5
Purpose				✳	
Structure				✳	
Language					✳
Knowledge				✳	

Reader & Task

- The vocabulary requirements of this piece are high; some prior knowledge is required.
- Provide a concept map that students can use to list the different points made by the letter writer.

Informational Text: Personal Essay

▶ **Focus** In this personal essay, students learn a new meaning for a word and recognize ways in which the writer shows enthusiasm for the subject.

▶ **Teaching Tips**

Before Reading
- Present the term *hacker* and discuss students' understanding of its meaning (generally regarded as negative).
- You might share examples of common acronyms, such as SCUBA (Self-Contained Underwater Breathing Apparatus) or DVD (Digital Video Disc).

During Reading
- Suggest that students summarize the main idea of each paragraph and describe how each provides information about the topic.
- Guide students to notice examples of text features, such as italics, boldface, words in all capital letters, and acronyms, and think about the purpose they serve.
- Direct students' attention to the photograph and ask, *How does the photo support the writer's attitude about Hacker Scouts?*

After Reading
- Have students explain what they think the phrase "think outside the box" means as it pertains to the theme of this essay.
- Encourage students to compare and contrast Hacker Scouts with other kinds of youth programs they know about.

Common Core Connections

RI.4.1, RI.4.2, RI.4.4, RI.4.5, RI.4.7, RI.4.8, RI.4.10 • RF.4.3, RF.4.4 • W.4.9, W.4.10 • L.4.1, L.4.2, L.4.3, L.4.4, L.4.5, L.4.6

Complexity Index

Quantitative: Lexile 930

Qualitative	1	2	3	4	5
Purpose			✳		
Structure			✳		
Language				✳	
Knowledge				✳	

Reader & Task

- Students who are familiar with local youth programs may more easily make connections with the program described in the essay.
- Tell students to identify evidence in the text that indicates this is a personal essay and point out the ways in which the writer shows enthusiasm for the topic.

Name _____ Date _____

At Don's Diner

What details make this story funny?

1 I am a clock. I hang on the wall behind the counter, above the cash
2 register. I'm an old timepiece, maybe a tad dusty around my edges.
3 But there's little that goes on in Don's Diner that escapes my notice.
4   Right now, my big hand is just past the six, and my little hand is
5 nearing the eight. And here, right on time, are Red Hat and Checkered
6 Jacket. They settle into their usual seats at the counter, and Red Hat
7 says what he always says. "Morning, Don, I'll have the usual." Don
8 nods, wiping his hands on a towel. He smiles at Checkered Jacket as he
9 sets two steaming cups of coffee before these two regulars.
10   "What'll it be for you this A.M., Pete? Oatmeal's good today."
11   "Nah," Checkered Jacket replies. "I'd rather have two looking at me,
12 wheat toast, and cheese grits."
13   And so it went for the usual parade of customers this morning. They
14 ordered their food, Don wiped his hands, coffee got poured. But later,
15 when both my hands are gathered around 12, a fellow in overalls
16 walks in. He perches himself on a corner stool. "Hey," he calls to Don.
17 "Do you folks serve duck here?"
18   Don, remembering the tasty
19 duck sausage on the lunch
20 menu, nods his head. Getting the
21 answer he's hoping for, Overalls
22 swivels on his stool and whistles
23 toward the diner's entrance. The
24 door swings open and in waddles
25 a plump duck. It proceeds to flap
26 up onto the stool beside him. "Hi
27 there!" the duck greets Don. "I'll
28 have some dry cereal and a side
29 salad, please."
30   Like I said, little goes on here
31 that escapes my notice.

Name _____ Date _____

At Don's Diner

▶ **Answer each question. Give evidence from the story.**

1 Who is Pete, and how would you describe his outfit? _Pete is in the_
Checkered jacket _____
_____

2 What routines does the clock notice at the diner? _____
_____
_____
_____

3 What makes this a humorous story? _____
_____
_____
_____

4 Which is the best meaning of *two looking at me* (line 11)?

○ A. the two hands of the clock   ○ C. two eggs, sunnyside up

○ B. a pair of customers   ○ D. two kinds of pie

Tell how you chose your answer. _____
_____

5 Which statement best explains the joke at the end of the story?

○ A. Ducks order lunch at diners.   ○ C. Overalls has a pet duck that can talk.

○ B. Diners serve all kinds of customers.   ○ D. *Serve duck* has an unexpected meaning.

What evidence in the text helped you choose your answer? _____
_____
_____
_____

Name _____ Date _____

The Greedy Chief
Legend From Hawaii

In what ways does Chief Hala'ea live up to his description?

1   Long ago, Chief Hala'ea ruled the Big Island. He was selfish and unfair
2   to his people. Each day at dawn, the local fishing crews would sail to sea,
3   work demanding hours filling their nets, and return at dusk with their
4   catch. But as they returned, Hala'ea paddled out to greet them. He never
5   brought a warm welcome, only a cruel demand: "Give me all your fish!
6   Your catch is mine!"

7   Weary crews had no choice but to obey. Then Hala'ea would host an
8   unruly feast solely for his friends and family. The gluttonous chief wasted
9   more food than twice as many guests could eat. Yet the fishermen and
10 their families always lacked enough for a decent meal.

11 Hala'ea's insensitive ways fueled silent resentment. Eventually the
12 workers could no longer permit the chief to seize all their fish. So they
13 held a secret meeting, where they hatched a plot to bring about a
14 change. When the sun rose the next day, the fishermen quietly reviewed
15 their plan. They prepared their canoes, readied their nets, and paddled
16 to sea. The yellowfin tuna, or ahi, were in season. Each canoe collected a
17 bountiful catch.

18 As usual, while heading back to the Big Island, they saw Hala'ea
19 paddling to meet them. As usual he demanded, "Give me all your ahi!
20 Your catch is mine!"

21 The crew in each canoe obeyed. They sailed alongside the chief's
22 canoe, surrounding it. Soon everyone began to toss the fresh ahi into
23 Hala'ea's canoe. The greedy chief cackled with glee as the sparkling fish
24 piled up. After each crew unloaded its ahi, it paddled quickly to shore.

25 In the frenzy, Hala'ea didn't
26 notice that his canoe was getting
27 weighted down. Soon the vessel
28 could no longer stay afloat. By
29 the time Hala'ea realized that he
30 and the ahi were sinking, it was
31 too late. He bellowed for help, but
32 his cries were lost in the waves.

Name _____ Date _____

Why Worms Live Underground

▶ **Answer each question. Give evidence from the folktale.**

1 What is the conflict between the ants and the worms? _____

_____

_____

2 What does Chief Eyo mean when he speaks of the creatures' *ways* (lines 3 and 13)?

_____

_____

3 Why do you think the ants won the contest so easily? _____

_____

_____

4 Reread the last sentence of the tale. Which word below means the opposite of *reluctantly* (line 28)?

○ A. slowly   ○ B. willingly   ○ C. cautiously   ○ D. fearfully

Tell how you chose your answer. _____

_____

_____

5 The storyteller describes that, during the contest, *the carpet came undone* (line 21). What actually happened?

○ A. The field opened up.   ○ C. The marching ants separated.

○ B. The worms slithered away.   ○ D. The witnesses wore out Chief Eyo's carpet.

What evidence in the text helped your choose your answer? _____

_____

_____

_____

Name _____ Date _____

Sour Grapes
Based on a Fable by Aesop

Why did the fox's problem make her bitter?

1   Vulpina the fox felt and heard her empty stomach growl. It
2   had been many days since she had caught anything to eat. All
3   the swift field mice outran her, while the clever rabbits stayed
4   stock still and silent deep in the brush. Vulpina couldn't even
5   manage to steal a plump hen from a farm or drag a delicious
6   duck from a pond. She began to fear that she would soon die
7   of starvation.
8   That night in her hungry wanderings, she stumbled upon a
9   lush garden. She snuck in for a close look and a serious sniff.
10 A sweet and juicy scent made her lightheaded with craving.
11 Following her nose, Vulpina gazed up. There, in the faint light of
12 the moon, she saw a twisty grape vine heavy with purple fruit.
13 Vulpina stared longingly at the bursting bunches, so ripe and
14 ready to be devoured.
15   Vulpina licked her chops and extended her agile body
16 upward. But the grapes hung far beyond her reach. She tried
17 balancing on her hind legs until she lost her footing. But there
18 was still no chance to reach the inviting grapes. So she gathered
19 her strength, inhaled, focused on her goal, and leapt as high
20 into the air as she could. She vaulted and sprang again and
21 again, but even the lowest bunch escaped her grasp.
22   Vulpina thought of other ways to grab the grapes. She tried
23 throwing rocks at the bunches to whack them loose. She tried
24 climbing the twisty vine, but the height made her dizzy. Neither
25 method brought success.
26   Soon Vulpina was too weary to jump or throw or climb any
27 more. In defeat, she hung her tail, turned her back, and slunk
28 out of the garden. "Rot, you miserable grapes!" she cried. "You're
29 not worth the bother. Who wants to eat sour grapes anyway?"

30 **Moral:** *Speaking ill of what you cannot have makes you sound bitter.*

Sour Grapes

▶ Answer each question. Give evidence from the fable.

1 Why was Vulpina so hungry? _Because she had not_ _catch any thing to eat._

2 What made the lush garden so inviting to Vulpina? _because she_ _didn't have to catch any thing just get grapes._

3 The phrase *sour grapes* comes from this ancient fable. In your own words, explain what you think this phrase means.

I think sour grapes means bad and not fit to eat.

4 Vulpina *licked her chops* (line 15) because she was _____.

○ A. lost   ○ B. tired   ○ C. dirty   ◉ D. hungry

Tell how you chose your answer. _licking your chops means your so hungry._

5 Which could be another way to state the moral of this fable?

○ A. Honesty is the best policy.   ○ C. Fools always mock what they cannot get.

◉ B. Appearances may be deceiving.   ○ D. There is always someone worse off than yourself.

What evidence in the text helped you choose your answer? _who wants to eat sour grapes anyway?_

Name _____ Date _____

Spy Museum

What makes this passage a fantasy?

1   "You all remember James Bond from the last century, don't you?"
2   asked the guide in the first room we entered. "Well, we've come a long
3   way spy-wise. 007 himself would be amazed. Let's first check out the
4   exploits of Special Agent 0027," she added. "He can change his size
5   whenever danger demands it!"
6   She then launched into a description of some of the jaw-dropping feats
7   attributed to 0027. For instance, one time he made himself particle-sized
8   and ruined a villain's attempt to set off a terrible bomb. The bomb never
9   exploded, a major city escaped disaster, and the villain's evil scientist
10   never understood what went wrong.
11   In a second room, we came face-to-face with a huge photo of Special
12   Agent 0044 at work. "He's an ordinary man except that he can change
13   forms," the guide explained. In this
14   photo, he'd turned himself into a
15   gigantic squid that draped itself around
16   a rogue nuclear sub and was wrestling
17   it to the ocean floor. Again, devastation
18   was avoided.
19   "I've saved the best for last," the guide
20   said with a sly grin as we entered the
21   third room. The special agent featured
22   here is 0082. "This agent's approach to
23   battling evil is to make herself invisible.
24   She slips into criminals' secret meetings,
25   unseen, and rewrites their dastardly
26   operation plans so that they will fail.
27   Amazing, right?"

28   I had no idea spies could do any of these things. Then, just as I was
29   imagining what kinds of special powers I would need to be a successful
30   spy, I heard my mother's voice. "Wake up Sam. Remember, today your
31   class is going to the Spy Museum to see its special exhibit: *What's New for
32   James Bond in 2014?* Get up, now."

Name _____ Date _____

Spy Museum

▶ **Answer each question. Give evidence from the fantasy.**

1 Who is telling this story? How do you know? _Sam because he's_ _saying things like she and we and I._ _____

2 What is similar about the abilities of Agents 0027, 0044, and 0082? _The all_ _stop evil vilians plans._ _____

3 What elements of this passage make it a fantasy? _When at the_ _end of the article it says "Wake up_ _Sam"._ _____

4 James Bond is the name of a _____.

○ A. former president   ○ B. tour guide   ○ C. villain   ◉ D. spy

What evidence in the text helped you choose your answer? _because he_ _was mentioned to be spy-wise._

5 Which of the following is an example of a *dastardly* (line 25) plan?

○ A. building a modern submarine

◉ B. inventing something to block out the sun and freeze the earth

○ C. having supernatural powers

○ D. becoming a nuclear scientist

What evidence in the text helped you choose your answer? _Because the_ _text gives examples of vilans_ _being or trying to do bad things_

Name _____ Date _____

Seneca Falls, 1848

What happened in Seneca Falls in 1848?

1   It was hot, bumpy, and noisy on the long train ride, but Grandma's
2   spirits were sky-high when the steam locomotive chuffed into the Seneca
3   Falls station. It was the summer of 1848. Grandma takes me wherever she
4   goes. So, I would be her companion the whole while at a unique event—a
5   convention devoted to women's rights. My grandmother wanted to push
6   back against what Elizabeth Stanton and others viewed as an "absolute
7   tyranny of men." Over and over Grandma had lectured me that women
8   in America did not enjoy the full rights of citizenship. "I'm tired of being a
9   second-class American," she'd complain.

10 I sat by her side, fidgeting and daydreaming, through endless debates
11 about changing the role of women in society. During one, frustrated that
12 I couldn't see past the head of the man sitting in front of me, I leaned
13 toward Grandma and muttered. "Of the 400 people here, why did the
14 tallest one have to sit right there?"

15 Overhearing my grumbling, that man chuckled and turned around. "I
16 am Frederick Douglass, son. Others before you have complained about
17 my big noggin." He offered his apology. Then he offered me his large,
18 powerful hand.

19 "He's a famous fighter against slavery," Grandma whispered to me once
20 the man had turned back around. "And he was once a slave himself."

21 Later, to Grandma's delight, the conference passed a critical
22 resolution—a call for voting rights
23 for women. This, she explained,
24 was a groundbreaking moment for
25 the women's suffrage movement.
26 There and then, Grandma
27 became one of our country's first
28 suffragettes.

29 On the ride home, she hugged
30 me. With tears of joy in her eyes,
31 she proclaimed that, together, we
32 had witnessed a turning point in
33 American history.

Name _____ Date _____

Seneca Falls, 1848

▶ **Answer each question. Give evidence from the story.**

1 Why is "absolute tyranny of men" (lines 6 and 7) set in quotation marks? _because_ _that is a quote for the conference._

2 How does the picture relate to the story? _The picture shows the conference stage and 2 women on it speaking to the awaiting crowd._

3 Why do you suppose that Frederick Douglass attended a conference on women's rights? _Because he's a fighter for equal rights._

4 *Suffrage* (line 25) is a word that means the right to _____.

○ A. vote   ◉ B. suffer   ○ C. speak in public   ○ D. be equal to men

Tell how you chose your answer. _because suffrage means_ _struggle or not doing well._

5 Which fact about Elizabeth Stanton does the text support?

○ A. Her home was in Seneca Falls.

○ B. She lectured the boy on women's rights.

○ C. She was a close friend of Frederick Douglass.

◉ D. She believed that women deserved more rights.

What evidence in the text helped you choose your answer? _my grandmother_ _wanted to push back against what_ _elizabeth stanton and others viewed as_ _an absoulte tyenny of men!._

Name _____ Date _____

Found at Last

What sensory details enrich this passage?

1   It was a relatively short hike, but at an altitude of 8,500 feet, my
2   cousin and I tired easily. The trail wove through a dense forest of
3   Ponderosa pine and Douglas fir. An occasional thicket of aspen with
4   rustling yellow leaves stood in striking contrast with the dark green
5   conifers and the black and gray volcanic rocks.
6   After an hour or so, we reached a clearing. There, we spotted
7   what appeared to be a broken-down shack. Behind it was a smaller
8   structure, possibly a storage shed. We eagerly approached.
9   Upon closer inspection,
10   we realized that we had
11   come upon a settler's
12   modest dugout. The cozy
13   cabin was constructed of
14   sod and wood and was
15   sunken into the ground. Its
16   roof, perhaps higher once,
17   sagged to a height of less
18   than three feet above the
19   ground. We ducked down
20   and crawled in.

21   On our knees, we found ourselves in a single windowless room that
22   was dark and musty. Once our eyes adjusted, we could detect some
23   simple furnishings. There was a rusted woodstove in one corner and
24   part of an iron bedstead along a wall. Next to it was the remains
25   of a battered trunk and, scattered on the dirt floor, some broken
26   dinnerware. A long rustic table filled the center of the room. Two legs
27   were broken, so the top was aslant, resting against the floor. Near it lay
28   a tattered book, which I snatched before we crawled out the way we
29   came in.
30   The book seemed to be a journal, but dampness and age had made
31   the words run together or disappear entirely. I couldn't decode much,
32   but am fairly certain I read the date **1884**, the name **Emma**, and the
33   words **found at last**.

25 Complex Text Passages to Meet the Common Core: Literature and Informational Texts, Grade 4 © 2014 by Scholastic Teaching Resources

Name _____ Date _____

Found at Last

▶ **Answer each question. Give evidence from the mystery.**

1 Use details from the text and the picture to describe a *dugout* (line 12). ___*A dugout*___
___*I Think is a small cabin.*___
_____
_____

2 Before finding the journal, what clues did the hikers notice about the age of the cabin?
___*It was very old and not very*___
___*open and close to civilation. I*___
_____

3 What makes the end of this story so puzzling? ___*because at The*___
___*end it says the date 1884 and name*___
___*emma and title found at last.*___

4 The most likely setting for this story is _____.

○ A. at the seashore ◉ B. in the mountains ○ C. in a desert ○ D. on an island

Tell how you chose your answer. ___*The picture makes my*___
___*answer clear.*___
_____

5 Which of these would be considered *rustic* (line 26)?

◉ A. an old computer ○ B. a woven basket ○ C. a Douglas fir ○ D. a pocket watch

What evidence in the text helped you choose your answer? ___*because This*___
___*huse is old so rustic must probuly*___
___*be a fany word meaning old.*___

Name _____ Date _____

Frogs on Logs

How is the information in the recipe organized to be helpful?

1 **Frogs on Logs**

2 Snack to serve 4–6

3 This snack may not be a dessert, but making it is a piece of cake!
4 It involves no cooking or baking, and very few ingredients. And
5 don't worry—no frogs are harmed or eaten, and not one tree must
6 be cut down. Yet the tasty results will whet your appetite and
7 make you smile.

8 **Ingredients**
9 • 4 stalks celery
10 • $\frac{1}{3}$ cup cream cheese
11 • 16 pimiento-stuffed green olives

12 **Utensils**
13 • dishtowel or paper towel
14 • cutting board
15 • cutting knife (adult use only)
16 • spreading knife
17 • serving plate

18 **Directions**
19 **1.** Wash and dry the celery stalks.
20 **2.** Fill each stalk with cream cheese.
21 **3.** Cut each filled stalk into two or
22   three "logs."
23 **4.** Slice the olives into disks.
24 **5.** Top each log with olive "frogs."

Name _____ Date _____

Frogs on Logs

▶ **Answer each question. Give evidence from the recipe.**

1 Why does the recipe call for two different kinds of knives? _____

_____

_____

2 Why are some words in **bold** type? How does this help a reader? _____

_____

_____

_____

3 Why are the directions numbered, but the ingredients and utensils are not? _____

_____

_____

_____

4 Which of the following are *utensils* (line 12)?

○ A. celery   ○ B. eggs   ○ C. strainers   ○ D. tablecloths

Tell how you chose your answer. _____

_____

5 Which means the same as *a piece of cake* (line 3)?

○ A. baked dessert   ○ C. good treat for a party

○ B. very simple to do   ○ D. part of the whole thing

What evidence in the text helped you choose your answer? _____

_____

_____

_____

_____

Name _____ Date _____

"Citizen" of the World

How does the author grab your attention in this piece?

1　　You find it the world over. In some cultures it has always been sacred.
2　In other cultures, it stands for cowardice or confusion. In many places,
3　it stands for patience and caring. And just about everywhere people
4　fry it, bake it, bread it, broil it, smother it in sauce, make soup with it,
5　cut it into salads, or tuck it between slices of bread. What is "it"? The
6　amazing chicken.

7　**Beginnings**　Chickens came originally from the warm, wet climates
8　of India and Southeast Asia. They were wild, flightless birds, and were
9　pretty easy to catch. Eventually, people kept and raised chickens. Later,
10　these domesticated birds were brought to different regions of the world.

11　**Better Birds**　The ancient Egyptians figured
12　out how to get hens to lay more eggs. The
13　ancient Romans came up with new ways
14　to cook the bird. In Rome, chicken became
15　a favorite main dish. In fact, it was such
16　a beloved food that the authorities got
17　concerned. In the interests of having people
18　live more humbly, they passed a law to limit
19　the eating of chicken to one meal a day.

20　**Broilers and Layers**　The chicken arrived
21　in North America well before Columbus
22　did. But until the 1900s, it played only
23　a small role in people's diets. Chickens
24　were mainly a source for eggs. Over time,
25　farmers began to breed *broilers* as well as
26　*layers*. Broilers are plump and meaty and
27　meant for eating. Today, chicken is the
28　most popular meat in America.

Name _____ Date _____

"Citizen" of the World

▶ **Answer each question. Give evidence from the magazine article.**

1 What did the ancient Egyptians do to improve chicken farming? _____ *They found*
_____ *a different way to cook chickens* _____
_____

2 What made wild chickens fairly easy to catch? _____ *They wouldn't*
fly and this made some
advantages to humans.

3 Why do you think the author put the word *citizen* in quotation marks in the title
of this piece?
_____ *Because citizen is saying that*
they respect them but they are
not human.

4 A *domesticated* (line 10) chicken is no longer _____.

⊙ A. wild ○ B. eaten ○ C. cooked ○ D. caught

Tell how you chose your answer. _____ *because domesticated*
animal is not wild.

5 Which statement about the chicken is true?

○ A. The chicken is an endangered bird.

⊙ B. Chickens are raised mainly to provide eggs.

○ C. Chickens have been around for thousands of years.

○ D. Chickens are more popular in America than anywhere else.

What evidence in the text helped you choose your answer? _____ *Chickens are*
mainly for a source of eggs.

Name _____ Date _____

The Apology

What can you tell about Marcus from his e-mail to Ms. Lopez?

1 From: MSINGH@ZTL.com
2 Date: Wednesday, June 5, 2014, 01:13 PM
3 To: Cindy Lopez

4 Subject: Class visit

5 Hi Ms. Lopez,

6 I am so sorry to inform you that we'll need to reschedule your class's visit
7 to my company. I've been looking forward to showing the kids what we
8 do here at TECHTOOLS. However, I've just learned that I'll need to be out
9 of town then to attend the New Tech Conference in Las Vegas. This was
10 unexpected and, I might add, not desired. (I've already told Lulu about
11 this unanticipated change of plans. Poor kid's pretty upset!)

12 But I have an idea that I hope might make things even more enriching
13 for your students when they do eventually come here. Here's my
14 suggestion. Ask the class to think of ideas for tools, gadgets, and apps
15 that they would like to see invented. Guide them to think about what
16 would make their everyday lives better. Have them use their wildest
17 imagination. We can then talk about these devices, some of which may
18 already be in the pipeline. What do you think? Good idea?

19 I'll have my assistant contact you. You can discuss new dates for your
20 visit. In the meantime, I'll be at meetings and more meetings for three
21 solid days. Ouch! You know, I'd much rather be one of your students now.
22 Then, instead of what I will be doing, I could be brainstorming ideas to
23 improve lives!

24 Again, please accept my sincerest apologies.

25 Thanks,
26 Marcus

Name _____ Date _____

The Apology

▶ **Answer each question. Give evidence from the e-mail.**

1 Why does Marcus need to apologize to Ms. Lopez? _becanse he was a meeting and Ms. Lopez's class can't visit._

2 Who is Lulu, and what clues help you know? _A student probably Marcus's son/daughter student flor of Ms. Lopez._

3 Describe the tone of this e-mail. What does it show about the kind of person Marcus is? _aphogizing and sorry._

4 The expression *in the pipeline* (line 18) means _____.

- ○ A. is in liquid form
- ◉ B. is already being worked on
- ○ C. is kept underground for safety
- ○ D. is ready to use

Tell how you chose your answer. _becanse using the evidence from the text._

5 Which statement about Marcus's trip to Las Vegas is true?

- ◉ A. It ends all chances students have to visit Techtools.
- ○ B. Marcus enjoys brainstorming at meetings.
- ○ C. Marcus looks forward to seeing friends at the conference.
- ○ D. Marcus would rather not have to travel out of town.

What evidence in the text helped you choose your answer? _because the students in Ms. Lopez's class can't visit Marcus's company._

Name _____ Date _____

Proposal for an Art Gallery

How does the speaker present and support his argument?

1   Ladies and Gentlemen,

2   Thank you for inviting me to the school board meeting. My name is
3   Devin Orth, and I'm in Mr. Kim's sixth-grade class. I'd like to propose
4   what I believe could be a terrific improvement to elementary schools
5   in our district.

6   My school has an empty classroom that is now used only for storage.
7   I think we should consider recycling it to meet a need we students
8   have. We need an art gallery. It would give us a place to display the
9   variety of art that we students create.

10 As you know, many of us paint, draw, make collages, sculpt, and
11 take photographs. We rarely get to share our art projects with a wider
12 audience. In a gallery space, we emerging artists could do just that.
13 I know that kids of all ages are making exciting art. A gallery of our
14 own would benefit our entire school community.

15 Our art teacher, Ms. Rosen, supports this idea. She would help set
16 things up and keep them going. And I know many students who would
17 happily volunteer to work in the gallery. I think we could open many
18 eyes. It wouldn't cost much, either.

19 I know that our community already has art museums and galleries.
20 But they feature the works of famous artists, all grown-ups. I think we
21 should get to enjoy the efforts of our not-so-famous artists, all kids.

22 Let's not lose this opportunity to enrich our school community by
23 engaging kids in art—not only doing it, but seeing and thinking about
24 it. What learning experiences this would provide! Imagine seeing your
25 own child's work hanging proudly as part of a well-organized display.

26 That empty classroom is sitting there, waiting. Thank you for listening.

Name _____ Date _____

Proposal for an Art Gallery

▶ **Answer each question. Give evidence from the speech.**

1 Who is the audience that Devin is addressing? _____

_____

2 What features of this passage show that it is a speech? _____

_____

_____

3 What details does Devin present to support his case for a student art gallery? _____

_____

_____

_____

_____

4 In this passage, to *propose* (line 3) means to _____.

○ A. volunteer   ○ B. suggest a plan   ○ C. ask someone to marry   ○ D. object to

Tell how you chose your answer. _____

_____

_____

5 Which is the best main idea for paragraph 3 (lines 10–14)?

○ A. Students like to display their art.

○ B. Not enough schools have art galleries.

○ C. The art program includes painting and drawing.

○ D. A student art gallery would improve the school community.

What evidence in the text helped you choose your answer? _____

_____

_____

_____

Name _____ Date _____

Choosing Groups

What is the purpose of this brochure?

1 ⭐ **Play It Cool After School** ⭐

2 **Activities for students in grades 3, 4, and 5**

3 Looking for something lively to do after school? Starting the week of
4 October 5, you can take part in a free activity program here at school.
5 Each activity group will meet on the same day of the week for 7 weeks.
6 Groups will meet from 3:15 P.M. to 4:45 P.M.
7 . Group size is limited to 20 students. Sign-ups will be *first come, first*
8 *served*. So speak with your family or caregiver. Decide which activity
9 group to join. Forms are due by September 24.

Mondays	Tuesdays	Wednesdays	Thursdays
Board Games	Dance Party	Computer Lab	Chess Club
Math Art	Kids Cook!	Chorus	Magic Tricks
Origami	Kite Making	Science Lab	Movie Time
Scrapbooking	History Club	Writer's Studio	Pottery

10 For more on each group, read the brief summaries below.

11 **Board Games** Play classic board
12 games, such as checkers, Clue, Kalah,
13 Monopoly, Othello, Parcheesi, Scrabble,
14 and others. There will be games for
15 two, three, four, or five players.

16 **Chess Club** Are you a beginner or an
17 experienced player? Come play chess
18 for the first time or improve your game
19 by learning new strategies and moves.

20 **Chorus** Is music one of your
21 favorite things? You will sing songs
22 in different languages from all over
23 the world.

24 **Computer Lab** Use the
25 computers for your own project, or
26 you can play learning games to
27 improve spelling, math, problem
28 solving, map skills, and more.

29 **Dance Party** Learn new dance
30 moves or practice ones you already
31 know. We'll roll up the rugs and
32 dance to mixed playlists!

33 **Kids Cook!** Do you love to mix,
34 measure, and create good things to
35 eat? Join this group to follow clear
36 and simple recipes for tasty treats.

Name _____ Date _____

Choosing Groups

▶ **Answer each question. Give evidence from the brochure.**

1 How would you explain the meaning of *first come, first served* (lines 7 and 8)? _____

_____

_____

2 Why is the sentence in line 9 underlined? _____

_____

_____

3 Compare and contrast how information about groups appears in the table and in
the summaries below it.

_____

_____

_____

_____

4 Another word for a *brochure* (opening question) might be _____.

○ A. an article   ○ B. a report card   ○ C. a catalog   ○ D. a summary

Tell how you chose your answer. _____

_____

_____

5 Which of these groups meets on Tuesdays?

○ A. Origami   ○ B. Pottery   ○ C. Chorus   ○ D. Kite Making

What evidence in the text helped you choose your answer? _____

_____

Name _____ Date _____

Balloon Wrangler

What does a balloon wrangler do?

1 Flori Ramos loves parades, especially ones
2 with huge balloons floating high above the
3 crowds. Flori interviewed Carlos, a balloon
4 wrangler in the Thanksgiving Day parade
5 in New York City. He was one of the many
6 people who helped fly Spider-Man.

7 **Q:** *Carlos, how did you get this job?*
8 **A:** I signed up almost a year ahead of time. There is no pay—it's a volunteer
9 job. You must be over 18, weigh at least 120 pounds, and be strong enough to
10 walk the entire parade route at a steady pace, no matter what the weather.

11 **Q:** *Did you get special training?*
12 **A:** I went to information sessions the organizers held earlier in the year.
13 We watched training videos, read instructions, learned safety rules, and
14 memorized hand signals. We got live practice in a football stadium a few
15 weeks before the big day.

16 **Q:** *How many wranglers work the ropes?*
17 **A:** That depends on a balloon's size and shape. Some balloons take as few as
18 40 wranglers, while others need as many as a hundred.

19 **Q:** *Does someone run each balloon crew?*
20 **A:** Sure. Each balloon has a 14-member flight team of pilots, captains, and
21 drivers. They are experts on geometry, balloon behavior, and safety. One
22 pilot marches first (but backwards the whole time!) to direct the team. The
23 other pilot walks last. Each captain directs up to 12 handlers. All the leaders
24 wear headsets to communicate. They give the wranglers directions using
25 hand signals. Two drivers steer a vehicle to secure each balloon.

26 **Q:** *Is safety a big concern?*
27 **A:** You bet it is! Each balloon can be five or six stories tall! Some are up to 60
28 feet long and 40 feet wide. Each team must control its balloon at all times so
29 it won't snag on trees or buildings, or tangle in wires or on lampposts.

Name _____ Date _____

Balloon Wrangler

▶ **Answer each question. Give evidence from the interview.**

1 How does the interviewer get information about the job of a balloon wrangler?

_____

_____

2 How is each question like a main idea? _____

_____

_____

_____

3 What do Flori's questions have in common? Explain how she has ordered the questions.

_____

_____

_____

4 Another term for balloon *wrangler* (line 4) is _____.

○ A. superhero   ○ B. cowboy   ○ C. handler   ○ D. pilot

Tell how you chose your answer. _____

_____

_____

5 What does Carlos mean by *the big day* (line 15)?

○ A. the day he signed up to be a balloon wrangler   ○ C. the day he will be interviewed

○ B. the first day of special training   ○ D. the day of the parade

What evidence in the text helped you choose your answer? _____

_____

_____

Name _____ Date _____

Remembering Mr. Rožak

In what ways did Mr. Rožak affect the author?

1 You never know when an experience may change you. I clearly
2 recall such a time. I was nine years old.

3 Our piano needed tuning, so my mother hired Mr. Rožak for the
4 job. As she guided him into our living room, I realized that Mr.
5 Rožak was blind.

6 He asked to be led to the piano. With his white cane, he explored
7 the floor nearby, seeking a spot for his toolbox. "Perfect!" he said
8 as he set down his box and opened it. It was divided into many
9 sections, each for a different type of tool. I'd never seen anything
10 arranged in such an orderly way.

11 When I asked if I could watch, he smiled
12 and nodded. So I sat nearby for the lesson of a
13 lifetime. Mr. Rožak opened the piano, exposing
14 its two hundred-some strings and tuning pegs.
15 Then he knelt at his toolbox to feel for specific
16 tools. He set them on a soft cloth he spread out
17 on the piano bench. As he worked, he returned
18 each tool to its exact spot. He asked for help
19 only once—to request some water. When he
20 finished tuning, he put the piano back together
21 and replaced each tool in its spot in his box.

22 "Mr. Rožak," I asked shyly, "why is your
23 toolbox so neat?"

24 "I learned when I was little that, although I
25 could not see, I had a good memory for space
26 and position," he explained. "I found that if
27 I organized my things carefully, I'd be able to
28 work as well as someone with two perfectly
29 good eyes."

30 Mr. Rožak gave me a new vision that I still
31 apply to this day. I arrange things—in my
32 desk, in the kitchen, in closets—so I can readily
33 find them.

Name _____ Date _____

Remembering Mr. Rožak

▶ **Answer each question. Give evidence from the memoir.**

1 Why did the family invite Mr. Rožak to their home? _____

_____

_____

2 Why do you think the writer was so interested in watching the piano tuner at work?

_____

_____

3 Explain how Mr. Rožak was able to put his tools back where they belonged. _____

_____

_____

4 Mr. Rožak began the tuning by *exposing* (line 13) the piano's strings and tuning pegs.
Another word for *exposing* is _____.

○ A. revealing   ○ B. adjusting   ○ C. protecting   ○ D. organizing

Tell how you chose your answer. _____

_____

5 Which best explains the *new vision* (line 30) the writer got by observing Mr. Rožak at work?

○ A. It is important to keep your piano tuned.

○ B. It is kind to allow others to watch as you work.

○ C. Having an orderly toolbox can be a useful thing.

○ D. Being organized can help you work more effectively.

What evidence in the text helped you choose your answer? _____

_____

_____

Name _____ Date _____

A Pet Plan?

What arguments does the writer use to persuade readers?

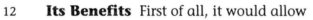

1   **My Plan** My dog, Pebbles, is home by
2   herself much of the day and no doubt gets
3   lonely. I bet your pets do, too. I propose
4   that it would be a fantastic idea and a rare
5   educational opportunity to bring them with
6   us to school!
7   Now, I don't mean all pets should come
8   every day. That could be noisy, distracting, or
9   even unsafe. But how about having one pet
10   in class at a time? We would surely benefit
11   from this experiment.

12   **Its Benefits** First of all, it would allow
13   us to study animals as scientists do. Our
14   class would learn some biology concepts by observing and describing
15   what we see, hear, feel, and smell. Like scientists, we could take notes
16   and compare observations. Also, we would get the chance to write
17   descriptively and to speak knowledgeably about what we notice or learn.
18   Although each pet owner would be responsible for the pet's care
19   during the school day, all of us would participate. That way, we all
20   would gain experience in tending to a living creature. What teacher
21   wouldn't want to give kids a chance to be observant? What parent
22   would oppose learning responsibility? What pet would object?

23   **Yes, but…** I know that some people will immediately disagree. But let
24   me assure doubters that I'm thinking of easy-to-mind pets like dogs, cats,
25   hamsters, birds, and turtles. I'm not suggesting that we invite pythons or
26   alligators to slither about. I also know that some kids are uncomfortable
27   around animals. Maybe my plan could help them overcome their fear.

28   **And so…** I believe that if we undertake this plan thoughtfully, we could
29   reap rich rewards. And we'd have an awesome time in the process!

Name _____ Date _____

A Pet Plan?

▶ **Answer each question. Give evidence from the essay.**

1 Why does the writer give reasons for *not* bringing pets to school as part of his argument?

_____

_____

2 Describe the tone of the writer's argument. _____

_____

_____

3 In what ways do the first and last paragraphs of this essay work together? _____

_____

_____

_____

4 What unique opportunity does the writer hope to bring about?

◯ A. The writer wants to become a scientist.

◯ B. The writer wants to help people choose pets.

◯ C. The writer wants kids to bring their pets to school.

◯ D. The writer wants to make students more observant.

What evidence in the text helped you choose your answer? _____

_____

_____

5 The opposite of *doubters* (line 24) would be _____.

◯ A. learners　　◯ B. nonbelievers　　◯ C. observers　　◯ D. supporters

Tell how you chose your answer. _____

_____

_____

Name _____ Date _____

Minor Miracle

How would you explain the title of this article?

1   **Chattanooga, TN, April 3, 1931**

2   Yesterday, the unthinkable

3   took place right here in our town.

4   Yankee stars Babe Ruth,

5   the "Sultan of Swat," and Lou

6   Gehrig, the "Iron Horse," were

7   in town. The Yankees, on their

8   way home from spring training

9   in Florida, stopped here to play

10   an exhibition game with our

11   AA minor-league team, the

12   Chattanooga Lookouts.

13   Ruth and Gehrig are two of the

14   best sluggers in baseball today.

(From left) Lou Gehrig and Babe Ruth watch Jackie Mitchell demonstrate her pitch.

15   Jackie Mitchell, on the other hand, is a 17-year-old girl who has just joined the

16   Lookouts. She is the only female player on the squad. To see how she would

17   do, the manager sent the young rookie to the mound to pitch.

18   The first batter Jackie faced was The Babe. Twice he swung and missed her

19   wicked curve ball. Then a pitch on the corner of the plate caught him looking.

20   *Strike three!* Ruth kicked the dirt, tossed away his bat, and angrily stomped

21   back to the dugout. Gehrig, the big first baseman, was up next. He fared no

22   better, swinging three times and hitting nothing but air. Two batters later,

23   Jackie's manager took her out. But what she did can never be undone.

24   That a young girl could strike out two giants of the game is huge news.

25   It made the sports pages of not only this newspaper, but also the *New York*

26   *Times* and *Daily News*. But the commissioner of major league baseball was not

27   impressed. In fact, he voided Jackie's minor-league contract, claiming that

28   professional baseball was too strenuous for women. What did Babe Ruth,

29   her first victim, have to say? He told reporters that women can't make it in

30   baseball because they are "too delicate."

31   Back to the dugout, Babe!

Name _____ Date _____

Minor Miracle

▶ **Answer each question. Give evidence from the newspaper article.**

1 What clues tell you that this is a newspaper article? _____

_____

_____

2 Describe Babe Ruth's reaction to being struck out. _____

_____

_____

3 Why did the writer give the article the title *Minor Miracle*? _____

_____

_____

4 A job that is *too strenuous* (line 28) is _____.

○ A. exhausting   ○ B. expensive   ○ C. relaxed   ○ D. unusual

Tell how you chose your answer. _____

_____

_____

5 The article says that the baseball commissioner *voided* (line 27) Jackie's contract.
What did he do?

○ A. He fired Jackie's manager.

○ B. He cancelled her agreement with the Lookouts.

○ C. He kept her from pitching to major league players.

○ D. He made her try out for the Yankees.

What evidence in the text helped you choose your answer? _____

_____

_____

Name _____ Date _____

Juan's Party

How will you use the calendar to solve a problem?

1   To celebrate his birthday, Juan wants to take five friends to a movie and
2 then to eat pizza. His birthday is on August 22, but he is willing to be flexible
3 about the date of the celebration. He has to be because in the summer, some
4 of his friends are unavailable. They either have commitments on certain
5 days or dates, or will be away for longer periods of time.
6   Juan has picked the movie, *A Giraffe's Tall Tale*, and the restaurant,
7 Emilio's. But selecting the date is problematic. Here's why choosing it will be
8 such a challenge.

9 • Amy can't attend on weekends or on Wednesdays.
10 • Bobby will be away from the 9th to the 16th.
11 • Carlos will be out of town during the last week of the month.
12 • Delia can never go on a Tuesday, and can't eat beans.
13 • Evie already has plans for Monday the 5th and for the Monday two weeks
14   after that.

15   Use the calendar to get a clearer picture of the challenges Juan faces as he
16 attempts to use logic to pick the date.

August

Sunday	Monday	Tuesday	Wednesday	Thursday	Friday	Saturday
				1	2	3
4	5	6	7	8	9	10
11	12	13	14	15	16	17
18	19	20	21	22	23	24
25	26	27	28	29	30	31

Name _____ Date _____

Juan's Party

▶ **Answer each question. Give evidence from the essay and table.**

1 What dates are not possible for Delia? _____

2 Which of Juan's friends could not attend on August 10? Explain. _____

_____

_____

3 On which dates might Juan hold his party? Explain how the calendar helps you decide.

_____

_____

_____

4 What does it mean to "have commitments on certain days or dates" (lines 4 and 5)?

○ A. The person is free to take part during those times.

○ B. The person already has other plans or things to do.

○ C. The person is not interested in going to the party then.

○ D. The person is on a committee that meets on those dates.

What evidence in the text helped you choose your answer? _____

_____

_____

5 Which is the best explanation for why a calendar is a kind of table?

○ A. It includes numbers.   ○ C. It organizes data into rows and columns.

○ B. It is in the form of a rectangle.   ○ D. You find one in almost every classroom in America.

Tell how you chose your answer. _____

_____

_____

Name _____ Date _____

Do-It-Yourself Lava Lamp

What text features help make the instructions easy to follow?

1 Lava lamps first made their appearance as a novelty item
2 in 1963. They didn't contain actual boiling lava from an
3 active volcano, but the liquid inside did move in much
4 the same slow, burbling manner as lava does as it inches
5 along. Now, you can make your own lava lamp with
6 simple materials you probably already have at home.

7 **Materials**
8 • funnel
9 • empty 16-oz. clear plastic water bottle with screw-on cap
10 • 10 oz. vegetable oil
11 • tap water
12 • food coloring in a dark color
13 • 1 large antacid tablet

14 **Step-by-Step Instructions**
15 **1.** Place the funnel in the bottle. Pour the
16   oil into the funnel. Then add water until
17   the bottle is almost full. Leave a little bit
18   of space.

19 **2.** Add 12 drops of food coloring. Swirl
20   gently to mix.

21 **3.** Break the antacid tablet into eight small
22   pieces. Drop one piece of the tablet into
23   the liquid. It will begin bubbling. When
24   the bubbling stops, add another piece.
25   Again, wait until the bubbling stops.
26   Repeat until you use all the pieces.

27 **4.** When the bubbling finally stops, screw
28   the top onto the bottle. Slowly tilt the
29   bottle from side to side. Look for the
30   blobby lava waves!

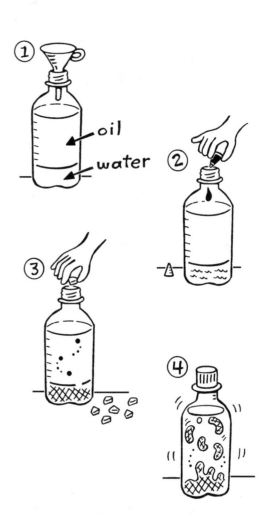

Name _____ Date _____

Do-It-Yourself Lava Lamp

▶ **Answer each question. Give evidence from the science activity.**

1 In Step 1, why do the instructions say to leave some space at the top of the bottle?

_____

_____

2 Explain why the activity includes two different lists. _____

_____

_____

3 Why do you think the instructions tell you to break the antacid tablet into eight small pieces? Explain.

_____

_____

_____

4 Which of the following things might you see *burbling* (line 4)?

○ A. meat cooling off   ○ C. oatmeal cooking

○ B. a potato baking   ○ D. ice cubes melting

Tell how you chose your answer. _____

_____

5 Based on the introduction and the picture, which best explains what *a novelty item* (line 1) is?

○ A. something invented at least 50 years ago

○ B. anything that can be used to provide light

○ C. a surprising new item people want to have

○ D. a scientific book, article, or project

What evidence in the text helped you choose your answer? _____

_____

_____

Name _____ Date _____

The Aztec Calendar

In what ways were the Aztec calendars unlike ours?

1　　　If someone asked you for today's date, you could answer easily. You
2　could state the day, month, date, and year. In short, your answer might be
3　something like Wednesday, January 9, 2014.
4　　　But if you had lived in central Mexico six centuries ago, that same
5　question might have been trickier to answer. At that time, your home
6　would have been part of the Aztec civilization that dominated large parts
7　of the region. You might have lived near where Mexico City is today. The
8　tricky part is that you would have used not one, but two, calendars! One
9　was sacred. It fixed the times of religious festivals. The other calendar was
10　agricultural. It showed the best times of year to plant.

11　**Sacred Calendar**　The Aztecs believed that their world
12　was the fifth one ever to exist. They called it a "sun." They
13　divided their sacred calendar into twenty 13-day weeks.
14　Each day was identified by a number from 1 to 13 and
15　one of 20 symbols of daily life. The numbers increased
16　each day from 1 to 13, after which they repeated. The
17　day count began with 1 and the Crocodile symbol, followed by 2-Wind,
18　3-House, and 4-Lizard. It continued up to 13-Reed, then the numbers
19　began again with 1 but continued with each of the remaining symbols in
20　turn, from the 14th symbol (Jaguar) to the 20th (Flower). The 20 symbols all
21　appear on a "Sun Stone," a wheel with a sun god
22　at its center. This "day count" calendar kept the
23　many Aztec gods happy. It gave each one a time
24　to rule and to be worshipped.

1-Crocodile

Aztec sun god

25　**Agricultural Calendar**　The other Aztec
26　calendar was more like our solar calendar. This
27　"year count" calendar had 20 months, each with
28　18 days. Each year also had five nameless days,
29　which were thought to be unlucky. Aztec babies
30　unfortunate enough to be born on a nameless
31　day remained nameless themselves until a named
32　day came around.

25 Complex Text Passages to Meet the Common Core: Literature and Informational Texts, Grade 4 © 2014 by Scholastic Teaching Resources

Name _____ Date _____

The Aztec Calendar

▶ **Answer each question. Give evidence from the article.**

1 In what part of the world did the Aztecs live? _____

_____

2 In what ways is the Aztec "year count" calendar like the one we use today? _____

_____

_____

_____

_____

3 Why do you think that both Aztec calendars feature the number 20? Explain. _____

_____

_____

_____

_____

4 The word *sacred* (line 9) means _____.

○ A. holy   ○ B. best   ○ C. worship   ○ D. famous

Tell how you chose your answer. _____

_____

_____

5 Which of these is an *agricultural* (line 10) product?

○ A. stone   ○ B. corn   ○ C. silver   ○ D. water

What evidence in the text helped you choose your answer? _____

_____

_____

Name _____ Date _____

Sail or Soar?

What does the title have to do with the purpose of this piece?

1   Wesley has saved a total of $38.46. His parents have given him
2   permission to spend up to $20 on anything he would like to reward
3   his successful saving. How can Wesley focus his shopping?
4   His sister Cara suggests that he purchase a model kit to put together
5   and display. This idea appeals to Wesley, who begins to browse dozens
6   of choices online. Since he enjoys history and building things, he
7   finally narrows the selection to two model kits: the Wright brothers'
8   first airplane or a replica of the HMS *Titanic*.
9   Wesley has read about the Wright brothers' historic flight in
10   1903. He's even seen a scratchy black-and-white film of another of
11   their flights. He also knows about the famous "unsinkable" luxury
12   ship that sank after hitting an iceberg in 1912. He'd be thrilled to
13   undertake either project. But since he has never built a model before,
14   he worries about getting in over his head.
15   Below are the details of the two models Wesley is considering.

Wright Flyer I	**HMS *Titanic***
Skill Level: medium+	**Skill Level:** beginner
Parts: 60	**Parts:** 92
Description: Plastic replica of biplane in which Orville Wright made the first powered flight. Paint and glue not included.	**Description:** 18-inch-long plastic model of ill-fated ship. Paint, glue, and string not included.
Customer Rating: ★ ★ ★ ★ ★	**Customer Rating:** ★ ★ ★ ★ ☆
Price $14.88 **Shipping** $ 2.75	**Price** $18.50 **Shipping** free

Name _____ Date _____

Sail or Soar?

▶ **Answer each question. Give evidence from the essay and table.**

1 Which kit earned the better customer rating? Explain. _____

_____

_____

2 Why might a *beginner* kit have more parts than a *medium+* kit? _____

_____

_____

3 How would you advise Wesley to use the data table to help him make his choice? Explain.

_____

_____

_____

4 A word from the text that means a *mock-up* or *close copy* is _____.

◯ A. reward   ◯ B. replica   ◯ C. biplane   ◯ D. display

Tell how you chose your answer. _____

_____

_____

5 If Wesley worries about *getting in over his head* (line 14), he might _____.

◯ A. not be able to reach something

◯ B. think he is a very capable person

◯ C. solve a hard problem without any help

◯ D. get stuck trying to do something too hard for him

What evidence in the text helped you choose your answer? _____

_____

_____

Name _____ Date _____

Chess Wonder

What made Josh Waitzkin's chess experience so unusual?

1 Chess demands strategy and creativity. Its greatest players can
2 visualize many moves in their minds to decide how to proceed. In the
3 chess world, some champions tower above all others. Greats like Garry
4 Kasparov, Bobby Fischer, and Magnus Carlsen lead this group.

5 **Happy Accident** Josh Waitzkin happened upon chess by accident.
6 When he was six years old, his mother took him to Washington Square
7 Park in New York City. There, on the way to the playground, they passed
8 pairs of men playing blitz chess. Their intense play captivated the boy.
9 Drawn to their rowdy, speedy game, Josh hung around, observing
10 everything. Soon, some of the men took notice of the young boy. As Josh
11 recalls, "My first teachers were street players, guys who would hustle
12 you…break you down mentally before they did it over the board."

13 **Chess Marvel** Most children would have felt overwhelmed,
14 but the challenge thrilled Josh. He soon became a pint-sized
15 chess marvel. "I didn't grow up learning chess or competing in a
16 protected environment," he recalls. "I grew up kind of in a raw
17 environment…life as a competitor is brutal."

18 **Champion** When Josh was seven, a professional chess coach
19 offered him formal lessons. Within two years, Josh had won
20 several national tournaments. He captured the National Junior
21 High Championship when he was in fifth grade. At the age of
22 ten, he defeated an adult chess master in only six moves. When
23 he was 11, he played to a draw in an exhibition game with
24 World Champion Garry Kasparov. Josh Waitzkin earned the title
25 of National Master when he was 13 years old. By 16, he was an
26 international chess master.

27 **At the Movies** You can get a glimpse into Waitzkin's early chess
28 life in the 1993 film *Searching for Bobby Fischer*. The movie was
29 based on a book written by Josh's proud father.

Name _____ Date _____

Chess Wonder

▶ **Answer each question. Give evidence from the biographical sketch.**

1 What was so unique about the chess match between Josh Waitzkin and Garry Kasparov?

_____

_____

2 What do you learn about Josh Waitzkin's personality from what he says about his own experiences?

_____

_____

_____

3 Summarize in your own words what was so amazing about Josh Waitzkin's chess accomplishments.

_____

_____

_____

_____

4 As used in this passage, those who *tower above all others* (line 3) must be _____.

○ A. very rare   ○ B. extremely tall   ○ C. highly talented   ○ D. champions

Tell how you chose your answer. _____

_____

5 Which means about the same as *played to a draw* (line 23)?

○ A. ended in a tie   ○ C. stopped before you were ready

○ B. had an art contest   ○ D. played with paper and pencil instead of chess pieces

How did you answer this question? _____

_____

Name _____ Date _____

Save the Majestic

What details does the writer use to persuade readers?

1   To the Editor:

2   I'm writing to respond to the recent
3   article supporting the immediate
4   demolition of the old Majestic Theater on
5   Main Street. I have an alternate proposal,
6   which I believe should be heard.
7   Decades ago, our mills and factories
8   worked at full speed. The lively streets of
9   our downtown bustled with activity as
10   residents and visitors strolled, gathered,
11   and window-shopped. Restaurants and
12   businesses thrived. Street lamps were festooned with seasonal decorations,
13   and our public parks were kept up beautifully. The grand Majestic was a
14   magnet for entertainment, featuring the latest Hollywood films and the
15   silliest cartoons.
16   Then came a rapid decline. The mills and factories began to lay off
17   longtime employees. Businesses closed their doors and shuttered their
18   windows, and the splendid Majestic fell to ruin. People began to desert our
19   once-vibrant downtown, leaving it forlorn.
20   We experienced difficult times, but they were yesterday. Today, stores
21   are reopening, new restaurants, shops, and galleries are settling in, and
22   other businesses are eager to follow. Our city is finally emerging from the
23   doldrums. With some forward-looking ideas, we can awaken our city again.
24   My proposal focuses on the magnificent Majestic. Let's put this elegant
25   old masterpiece of a building back on the map. If it is restored and
26   modernized, it could lead our economic turnaround. I urge renovating this
27   grand structure. Let's fling open its doors again, but not for films—it's far too
28   cavernous for today's moviegoers. However, it is perfect for plays, musicals,
29   concerts, dance performances, graduations, and rallies.
30   The future of the Majestic rests with all of our citizens. Let's cooperate with
31   enthusiasm to consider this option.
32   —Bailey Arsham

Name _____ Date _____

Save the Majestic

▶ **Answer each question. Give evidence from the letter to the editor.**

1 What does the writer hope will happen to the Majestic? _____

_____

_____

_____

2 The writer says, "We experienced difficult times, but they were yesterday" (line 20).
Explain what this statement means.

_____

_____

3 Describe the tone of this letter. What does it say about the writer's view of the city?

_____

_____

4 A synonym for *festooned* (line 12) is _____.

○ A. lit up   ○ B. painted   ○ C. draped   ○ D. enclosed

Tell how you chose your answer. _____

_____

5 Why did the Majestic Theater close its doors?

○ A. It was too big for movie audiences.

○ B. The nearby parks were in ruins.

○ C. The ticket prices were set too high.

○ D. During hard times, people had less money to spend.

What evidence in the text helped you choose your answer? _____

_____

_____

_____

Name _____ Date _____

Hacker Scouts

How does this essay offer a different view of hackers?

1 When you hear the term *hacker*, you picture a tech-savvy person
2 breaking into someone's computer to make trouble. So I scoffed at
3 Hacker Scouts, thinking they were just some mischief-makers. But I was
4 totally wrong! Since joining Hacker Scouts, I'm so excited about it that
5 I'm eagerly spreading the word.
6 Hacker Scouts is a youth program for kids 8–14 years old. A "hacker"
7 starts with something, learns how it works, and then makes it better.
8 I LOVE this idea! The program, which began in 2012, attracts do-it-
9 yourself kids who enjoy creating and making things with their hands.
10 It's based on STEAM learning, which mixes **S**cience, **T**echnology,
11 **E**ngineering, **A**rts, and **M**ath in cool activities.
12 Hacker Scouts learn by doing. We explore and apply skills of all
13 sorts, such as robotics, sewing, bicycle mechanics, video game creation,
14 electronics, and woodworking. We take old junk and hack it for new and
15 useful purposes. We salvage and tinker with just about anything that can
16 develop our minds and lets us work with our hands. For instance, I've
17 used the yarn from an old sweater to knit a hat and have built a talking
18 stuffed animal from a torn quilt for my sister. And hey, I'm only ten!
19 Everything we do in Hacker Scouts brightens my brain. I'm getting
20 good at using anything at hand. I've used tools, like a soldering iron,
21 that I thought were only for adults.
22 I'm learning from my errors
23 how to do better next time. We
24 Hacker Scouts are getting better at
25 listening and cooperating. Plus,
26 our leaders cheer us on to question
27 and think outside the box.
28 Joining the Hacker Scouts is free
29 and open to anyone, but so far is
30 available in only a few areas. I'm
31 lucky we have Hacker Scouts here
32 in Oakland, California.

Hacker Scouts Atticus (left) and Amelia (right)
at work soldering circuit boards

25 Complex Text Passages to Meet the Common Core: Literature and Informational Texts, Grade 4 © 2014 by Scholastic Teaching Resources

Name _____ Date _____

Hacker Scouts

▶ **Answer each question. Give evidence from the essay.**

1 What do Hacker Scouts do? _____

_____

_____

_____

2 Why are the words LOVE (line 8) and STEAM (line 10) written in capital letters? Explain.

_____

_____

3 Summarize what Hacker Scouts gain by taking part in this program. _____

_____

_____

_____

4 Which best describes the writer's attitude?

◯ A. puzzled   ◯ B. enthusiastic   ◯ C. humorous   ◯ D. serious

Tell how you chose your answer. _____

_____

_____

5 Which might you say if you *scoffed* (line 2) at an idea?

◯ A. "That's really not such a bad idea, I guess."   ◯ C. "You can't possibly be serious!"

◯ B. "This is the best idea I ever heard!"   ◯ D. "I already heard that one."

What evidence in the text helped you choose your answer? _____

_____

_____

Literature Passages

Passage 1: At Don's Diner

1. Sample answer: Pete is the first name of a regular customer. He always wears a checkered jacket (lines 8–10). **2.** Sample answer: Certain customers arrive at the same times and order the same foods, and Don always wipes his hands on a towel, takes orders, pours coffee, talks to people (lines 5–14). **3.** Sample answer: It's funny to have a clock telling the story, and describing the scene from its odd point of view. It's also funny and surprising that the duck isn't something on the menu, but a talking customer (lines 1–3, 23–29). **4.** C; Sample answer: There's talk about breakfast foods, so I thought of a breakfast food, and the yolks of two eggs look like eyes staring up from the plate (lines 10–12). **5.** D; Sample answer: D gets at the surprise—*serve duck* sounds at first like it means having a duck dish you can order, but here it means serving *to* a duck (lines 17–20, 23–29).

Passage 2: The Greedy Chief

1. Sample answer: He paddled out to meet them, only to demand that they give their entire catch to him (lines 4–6). **2.** Sample answer: It means that their work was hard and tiring, and they worked from dawn to dusk (lines 2–4). **3.** Sample answer: They acted with respect, as they always did, but knew that the giant catch would be too much for the chief's canoe. His own greed brought him down (lines 21–32). **4.** A; Sample answer: The crews were angry with the chief, so when they had a secret meeting, I knew they were making a plan to get even (lines 11–14, 21–32). **5.** C; Sample answer: The story doesn't exactly say why his cries were lost in the waves (meaning nobody heard them). But I know that the crews rowed back to land (line 24), and probably couldn't hear the cries. Also, the chief's boat was sinking (lines 27–31), and his cries stopped when he sank under the water (31–32).

Passage 3: The Courage Vault

1. Sample answer: Mr. Lin, the P.E. teacher, is cheerful, supportive, and encouraging (lines 3–5, 21–26). **2.** Sample answer: He wanted a student to demonstrate that it was possible for kids to do this vault (lines 11–12). **3.** Sample answer: Greta usually likes P.E. class, but fears the vault she knows she'll have to do. But after seeing other students succeed, and with Mr. Lin's help, she overcomes her fear, does the vault, and feels proud (lines 1–9, 14–31). **4.** B; Sample answer: Greta started out worrying about the courage vault, so I think it means she was afraid of it (lines 8–9). **5.** D; Sample answer: D is exactly how I picture Greta as she worked up her courage to do the vault. She did all the steps but stopped, just before jumping, until Mr. Lin helped her (lines 15–20).

Passage 4: The Peddler and the Trout

1. Sample answer: He says it can cure baldness (line 7). **2.** Sample answer: The trout became harder to catch, so they needed another method (line 15). **3.** Sample answer: "The trout took notice, especially the ones whose hair had grown too long or whose beards slowed them down. Those hairy trout leapt right out of the water up onto the banks for the free service" (lines 19–25). In real life, fish wouldn't grow hair or beards and need a shave. So, to describe hairy trout like it's ordinary is an example of tall tale silliness. **4.** D; Sample answer: Anglers were people trying to catch fish (lines 15–18, 25–27). **5.** C; Sample answer: The peddler spilled hair tonic into the stream (lines 12–13). Trout grew hair (lines 19–22).

Passage 5: Why Worms Live Underground

1. Sample answer: The worms got insulted by the ants boasting about their strength at the feast with Chief Eyo (lines 5–10). **2.** Sample answer: He understands that different creatures have their own kinds of habits, strengths, abilities, and ways of living. **3.** Sample answer: They showed organization, cooperation, attention, and planning to beat the worms. Their teamwork made the difference (lines 15–24). **4.** B; Sample answer: A, C, and D are closest in meaning to *reluctantly*—the worms are scared and don't want to come out! So, *willingly* is the best choice (lines 27–29). **5.** C; Sample answer: The marching ants are described as "flowing along the ground as a rippling brown carpet" (line 18). So, to attack, they broke apart to go after the worms (lines 21–22).

Passage 6: Sour Grapes

1. Sample answer: She had been unable to catch any creatures to eat (lines 1–7). **2.** Sample answer: The juicy grapes looked and smelled so tasty that she thought they would make a nice meal for her (lines 9–14). **3.** Sample answer: When you can't have something you want, your frustration may turn you against it. You pretend that you don't care, but you really do (lines 26–30). **4.** D; Sample answer: I knew that Vulpina was starving when she saw the grapes, so she licked her chops to show that she was very eager for food (lines 1–2, 6–7, 10). **5.** C; Sample answer: The tale is not about honesty or appearances. There might be another worse off than Vulpina, but C most closely fits the fable because Vulpina says, "Who wants to eat sour grapes anyway?" (lines 28–29).

Passage 7: Spy Museum

1. Sample answer: The storyteller is Sam, a boy who has woken up from a dream about going to a Spy Museum (lines 30–32). **2.** Sample answer: Each can change in some amazing and dramatic way in order to fight crime (lines 3–18, 21–26). **3.** Sample answer: The special agents can do things that are impossible in real life (lines 4–26). They come from the future (line 1), way after James Bond, who is still a character of today. In the end, these agents existed only in a boy's imagination while dreaming (lines 30–32). **4.** D; Sample answer: In Sam's dream, the tour guide refers to James Bond when she says "spy-wise" as she begins the tour (lines 1–3). **5.** B; Sample answer: I figured out that *dastardly* means evil or harmful, because lines 22 and 23 talk about 0082's "approach to battling evil," so I looked for an example of a really bad thing to do. The other choices are good things.

Passage 8: Seneca Falls, 1848

1. Sample answer: Those four words were the exact words that someone said. **2.** Sample answer: The picture shows a woman in old-fashioned clothing speaking on a stage in front of an audience and the sign behind her says, "National Women's Suffrage." It relates to the story, which is about the 1848 convention for women's rights (lines 3–5).

3. Sample answer: Douglass fought against slavery, which shows that he believed in equal rights for people who did not yet have them (lines 19–20). **4.** A; Sample answer: In the same paragraph, the author talks about a call for voting rights (lines 21–23). **5.** D; Sample answer: Grandma tells the boy about Stanton's views on women's rights (lines 5–9).

Passage 9: Found at Last

1. Sample answer: A dugout is a small, simple cabin built partly under the ground (lines 12–15). **2.** Sample answer: It must have been old because it was only one room, had no windows, and the roof was sinking down. It had a dirt floor, a wood stove, and most of the things inside were broken or rusty. There were no modern items (lines 9–29). **3.** Sample answer: You don't know who or what was *found at last*, who wrote the journal, or who Emma was, and you'll probably never know. **4.** B; Sample answer: It takes place in a forest that is at a high altitude, which sounds like mountains (lines 1–5). **5.** B; Sample answer: The cabin was from olden times and was built using natural materials that were available. The table was probably made by hand using wood from a tree. So, I think *rustic* means something that is plain, handmade, and country-like, not just old, so a woven basket is the best choice.

> ### Informational Text Passages

Passage 10: Frogs on Logs

1. Sample answer: You need a spreading knife for cream cheese (line 20), but a sharp knife to cut celery and olives (lines 21–23). **2.** Sample answer: They are headings that tell you what kind of information is just below. They help you see and understand the different parts of a recipe really easily (lines 8, 12, 18). **3.** Sample answer: You must follow the directions in the order given or the recipe won't turn out right; but you can collect ingredients and utensils in any order, as long as you get them all (lines 18–24). **4.** C; Sample answer: I see that utensils are tools and supplies used when cooking or preparing food (lines 12–17). **5.** B; Sample answer:

This is an expression that means something is easy to do. The clue is that this recipe has few ingredients (lines 8–11), only a few steps (lines 18–24), and needs no cooking (line 4).

Passage 11: "Citizen" of the World

1. Sample answer: The ancient Egyptians figured out how to get hens to lay more eggs (lines 11–12). **2.** Sample answer: They could not fly (lines 8–9). **3.** Sample answer: Chicken is a "citizen" of the world because it is a part of most cultures, and is found all over (lines 1, 7–8, 11–14, 20–22). But it's not a person, so it can't really be a citizen. **4.** A; Sample answer: I connected the word *domesticated* with "people kept and raised chickens" (line 9). **5.** C; Sample answer: The article says that ancient Egyptians and Romans had chickens and I know that the word *ancient* means a long, long time ago (lines 11–14).

Passage 12: The Apology

1. Sample answer: He must postpone a class visit to his company because he just found out he has to be away that day (lines 6–9). **2.** Sample answer: Lulu is a kid, probably Marcus's daughter and a student in Ms. Lopez's class. I know this because Marcus already told Lulu, and she got upset (lines 10–11). **3.** Sample answer: The tone is friendly, like a conversation, and it shows that Marcus is truly sorry to cancel. He cares about the kids, doesn't like having to disappoint them, and is helpful to the teacher (lines 6–24). **4.** B; Sample answer: Techtools looks for new ideas, so some of the good ones students come up with may already be in production (lines 14–18). **5.** D; Sample answer: Marcus complains about all the meetings (lines 20–21), and says the trip is not desired (lines 8–10). He also directly says he wishes he could stay home coming up with great ideas to make lives better (lines 22–23).

Passage 13: Proposal for an Art Gallery

1. Sample answer: He is speaking to members at the school board meeting (line 2). **2.** Sample answer: It begins by greeting an audience, the speaker introduces himself (lines 1–3), and at the end, he thanks his listeners (line 26). **3.** Sample answer: He

tells how the idea came to him (lines 6–9), why it makes sense (lines 10–14), who could help (lines 15–17), and the good it could bring (lines 20–25). **4.** B; Sample answer: I thought about the point of this speech, which was to offer a good idea for the empty classroom. He says "we should consider recycling it," which sounds like he will present them with a plan for using the room (line 7). **5.** D; Sample answer: The last sentence in the paragraph could be the topic sentence, so D is closest (lines 8–9, 22–25).

Passage 14: Choosing Groups

1. Sample answer: It means that groups fill up in order of how people reply. Groups can have only 20 students, so if you wait too long, you might not get into the group you want (line 7). **2.** Sample answer: It's a way to highlight an important date—a piece of information not to miss. **3.** Sample answer: Both sections tell what groups you could join. The table organizes groups alphabetically by the day they meet; the summaries are alphabetical and give a little more information about each group (table, lines 11–36). **4.** C; Sample answer: It's most like a catalog because it gives information about choices you can make. **5.** D; Sample answer: I looked down the Tuesdays column of the table until I found which group was listed there.

Passage 15: Balloon Wrangler

1. Sample answer: She asks questions of someone who holds that job and shares the answers (lines 7–29). **2.** Sample answer: Everything in the answer relates directly to that question. **3.** Sample answer: Each question gives Carlos a chance to tell what he knows about a part of the job of balloon wrangling. They are sort of in time order—they start with how he got the job, was trained, how each crew works, and their biggest concern (lines 7, 11, 16, 19, 26). **4.** C; Sample answer: The word *handler* is also used to refer to the job Carlos does (line 23). **5.** D; Sample answer: Carlos has been learning and preparing for his job, so the big day is when he will actually do it (lines 12–15).

Passage 16: Remembering Mr. Rožak

1. Sample answer: Their piano needed tuning, and he was a piano tuner (lines 3–4). **2.** Sample answer: The writer was curious about the process of tuning a piano as well as how someone who was blind would be able to manage it (lines 11–13, 22–23). **3.** Sample answer: He memorized the placement and position of each tool in his very organized toolbox (lines 8–10, 17–21, 24–29). **4.** A; Sample answer: He opened the piano to reveal the parts inside so he could tune them (lines 13–14). **5.** D; Sample answer: In the last paragraph, the writer explains the value of being organized.

Passage 17: A Pet Plan?

1. Sample answer: The writer wants to show that he or she understands other points of view, but believes he or she can show why his or her points are stronger (lines 7–11, 23–27). **2.** Sample answer: I think the writer is trying to persuade in a friendly and funny way, knowing that the plan may be turned down, but wanting to make the case anyway (lines 3–6, 22, 25–26). **3.** Sample answer: The writer begins and ends the essay by stating his or her main argument. The writer repeats the argument at the end, but closes with enthusiasm (lines 1–6, 28–29). **4.** C; Sample answer: The first and last paragraphs make the writer's views very clear. **5.** D; Sample answer: In line 23, the writer begins by saying: "Yes but..." The writer accepts that people may not be sure they like the idea of pets in school. So these people would be *doubters*. The opposite is *supporters*, people who would think this is a good idea.

Passage 18: Minor Miracle

1. Sample answer: It says "not only this newspaper, but also the *New York Times* and *Daily News*," which are both newspapers (lines 25–26). Plus, it looks like a newspaper article. **2.** Sample answer: He kicked dirt, threw his bat, and stomped to the dugout. This shows that he seemed furious and frustrated, maybe even embarrassed (lines 20–21). **3.** Sample answer: Jackie pitched for a minor league team, and what she did was so unbelievable it might be called a baseball miracle (lines 7–12, 15–16, 18–22). **4.** A; Sample answer: In lines 29 and 30, it says that Babe Ruth thought women were "too delicate," so I figured

that *strenuous* means too hard on the body and they would tire out easily. **5.** B; Sample answer: He was not impressed by what Jackie did and claimed that baseball was too hard for her (lines 26–28). But I think the real reason was because he thought Jackie had embarrassed the two famous baseball players.

Passage 19: Juan's Party

1. Sample answer: Delia cannot attend on August 6, 13, 20, or 27 because they are Tuesdays (line 12, calendar). **2.** Sample answer: August 10 is a Saturday. Amy can never attend on weekends, and Bobby will be away for a week, starting the day before that (lines 9–10). **3.** Sample answer: I crossed out every date when somebody couldn't attend (lines 9–14). After I did that for all five friends, I saw that the party could be on August 1, 2, 8, 22, or 23 (calendar). **4.** B; Sample answer: In lines 4 and 5, it says that some of his friends are unavailable either because they have commitments or will be away. When I looked at lines 9–14, I saw that some kids would be away, but others would be busy doing other things. So, I think *commitments* are plans already made that you can't change, so you should pick a different date. **5.** C; Sample answer: I know that a table is a chart with data. Calendars show how days and dates line up.

Passage 20: Do-It-Yourself Lava Lamp

1. Sample answer: There are more ingredients to be added (lines 19–26). **2.** Sample answer: The first list gives the materials you need for the project. The numbered list tells you the steps to follow in order. **3.** Sample answer: A big antacid tablet might not fit through the top of the soda bottle. And step 3 says to add one piece at a time and wait for the bubbling to stop before adding the next one. Maybe it has to do with what the bubbling does, and a whole tablet at once might bubble over (lines 21–26). **4.** C; Sample answer: I imagined lava burbling, which made me think of thick bubbles in slow motion. So, I picked oatmeal cooking because that's what you see when you make it on a stove. **5.** C; Sample answer: The picture at the top and the introduction gave me the idea that a lava lamp was something new and fun that people liked.

Passage 21: The Aztec Calendar

1. Sample answer: The Aztecs lived in central Mexico, maybe near what is now Mexico City (lines 4–7). **2.** Sample answer: Both calendars have about the same number of days. Both are based on the sun. Both have days and months (lines 25–28). **3.** Sample answer: The passage says that the Aztecs wanted to make their many gods happy. And both calendars gave each one a time to rule (lines 22–24, 26–28). So, I think they used the number 20 to honor their 20 important gods. **4.** A; Sample answer: In line 9, it says that the sacred calendar had to do with religious festivals, so *holy* is the best answer. **5.** B; Sample answer: Agriculture is about farming, so I picked the product that grows on a farm, corn. Also, the passage talks about the best times of year to plant (line 10).

Passage 22: Sail or Soar?

1. Sample answer: The Wright Flyer I. The plane got five stars, while the HMS *Titanic* got only four (table). **2.** Sample answer: The parts in the beginner kit might be bigger, easier to work with, or simpler to connect than the parts in the medium+ kit. **3.** Sample answer: The table shows five categories of data he can compare: skill level, number of parts, description, customer rating, and price. I might tell him to pick the easier model, since he's a beginner at model building himself. **4.** B; Sample answer: The word *replica* was used to describe the model kit of the *Titanic* (line 8) and the Wright Flyer I (table: Description section). Since I know a model is like a close copy, I figured *replica* means the same thing. **5.** D; Sample answer: Wesley has never built a model kit before, so he probably doesn't want to pick one that might be too difficult (lines 13–14). So, being worried about *getting in over his head* means he's worried that it's too hard.

Passage 23: Chess Wonder

1. Sample answer: Kasparov was a World Champion and Josh was just a boy of 11, but Kasparov couldn't beat Josh (lines 3–4, 22–24). **2.** Sample answer: I think Josh must have been curious, tough, competitive, and smart, despite his young age (lines 8–10, 11–12, 14–17). **3.** Sample answer: Josh began playing chess by accident at a very young age, not with a teacher but by watching adults playing in the park (lines 6–12). He was a fast learner who rose quickly to become a famous champion player while still a teenager (lines 24–26). **4.** C; Sample answer: In the first paragraph, the author mentions some of the greatest chess champions of all time. So, I think the best answer is C. They are far better than other champions. **5.** A; Sample answer: I knew that *draw* didn't mean make a picture in this case, and the rest of the paragraph talks about how well he did. So, to tie with a world champion would be a big accomplishment.

Passage 24: Save the Majestic

1. Sample answer: The writer wants it to be saved and remodeled to be used for other kinds of events (lines 24–29). **2.** Sample answer: Bad times happened in the past, but that's over, and now things are looking up. The writer talks about stores, restaurants, and galleries opening and that the city is coming out of the doldrums (lines 20–23). **3.** Sample answer: The tone is positive. The writer seems to love the city and feel bad to see a fine old theater disappear. The writer tries to convince readers that the Majestic is worth saving and will help make the city better again (lines 12–15, 17–19, 24–31). **4.** C; Sample answer: I pictured decorations hanging from street lamps on city streets, so I think C is the best answer. **5.** D; Sample answer: The writer describes hard times after the factories and mills closed, so D is best (lines 16–19).

Passage 25: Hacker Scouts

1. Sample answer: They learn about how things work to try to make them better, or they take old stuff and reuse it in new ways (lines 6–7, 14–15). **2.** Sample answer: The writer capitalizes LOVE to show excitement. STEAM is in capitals because each of its letters stands for a different word: Science, Technology, Engineering, Arts, Math. **3.** Sample answer: They learn to be inventive, to work with their hands, work in teams, and think creatively to try new things (lines 12–16, 19–27). **4.** B; Sample answer: The writer is very excited about Hacker Scouts (lines 4–5, 8, 19). **5.** C; Sample answer: The writer first thought that hackers could only be troublemakers, so becoming a hacker wouldn't be an idea you take seriously (lines 1–3).